Pearson
PUBLISHING

Consultation in the Classroom

Developing Dialogue about Teaching and Learning

Madeleine Arnot, Donald McIntyre,
David Pedder and Diane Reay

Further copies of this publication may be obtained from:

Pearson Publishing
Chesterton Mill, French's Road, Cambridge CB4 3NP
Tel 01223 350555 Fax 01223 356484
Email info@pearson.co.uk Web site www.pearsonpublishing.co.uk

ISBN: 978 1 85749 849 3

Published by Pearson Publishing 2004
© Pearson Publishing 2004
First published 2004
Reprinted 2007

Contents

Acknowledgements

We are grateful to the five schools which very kindly allowed their busy lives to be further complicated by letting us conduct the two research projects reported in this book. We are especially grateful to the teachers and pupils who, for the sake of this research, worked hard to reveal their classroom experiences and thinking to us. We owe a particular and exceptional debt to those pupils who at our request went further and shared their thoughts about teaching and learning with their teachers, and to those teachers who worked to change their teaching in the light of these pupils' thoughts. All the names we use for teachers and pupils are fictitious in order to protect their anonymity.

The planning and completion of the two research projects and the writing of this book have in very large measure been the outcome of Jean Rudduck's vision, as Director of the ESRC/TLRP Consulting Pupils about Teaching and Learning Project and as Series Editor, and of the sustained support, encouragement and guidance she has given us. If, as we hope, this is a helpful and thought-provoking book, then much of the credit for that must go to Jean.

We all owe a lot to the wider team of people we worked with. Beth Wang collected much of the data from one of the secondary schools in the second project. Our colleagues in the Consulting Pupils Project – Sara Bragg, Nick Brown, Nichola Daily, Helen Demetriou, Michael Fielding, Julia Flutter, John MacBeath and Kate Myers – have been an ongoing source of intellectual excitement and practical help.

Other titles in the series

Some issues that are not discussed in this book – for instance, student-as-researcher initiatives, different ways of consulting pupils – are covered in the other two publications in the series; all three are outcomes of the ESRC/TLRP Project, *Consulting Pupils about Teaching and Learning*:

Fielding M and Bragg S (2003) *Students as Researchers: Making a Difference*

MacBeath J, Demetriou H, Rudduck J and Myers K (2003) *Consulting Pupils: A Toolkit for Teachers*

Professor Madeleine Arnot, Professor Donald McIntyre and Dr David Pedder are from the Faculty of Education, University of Cambridge; Professor Diane Reay was at King's College, London and is now at the University of North London.

Professor Jean Rudduck, Series Editor, is also from the Faculty of Education, University of Cambridge.

1 Important questions about consultation

Donald McIntyre

An increasing number of people seem to accept that school pupils should be consulted about the provision that their schools make for them. For example, school councils on which pupils from all year groups are represented are more and more widespread and are being taken increasingly seriously. They can be seen not only as taking account of pupils' rights as consumers but also as a key element in the education of people learning to be citizens of representative democracies. Consultation of pupils has, furthermore, extended into classrooms. School pupils are being encouraged to believe that they are entitled to something of a voice in their affairs.

Our aim in this book is to contribute, on the basis of our research, to debate about how the voice of school pupils can appropriately contribute to the work of schools. While enthusiastically endorsing the general principle that pupils are entitled to have their voices heard, we believe that what that can fruitfully and justly mean in practice is far from a simple matter. Our particular concern here is with consultation with pupils about how their teaching and learning in classrooms might be improved. In one respect, our agenda is therefore more radical than most of the pupil consultation in schools today. Not only is our focus on classroom teaching and learning but, in addition, our concern is with pupils' own perspectives on classroom teaching and learning. We want to know how their understandings, their perspectives and their suggestions can contribute to the quality of classroom learning and teaching. In another respect, however, our agenda and our enthusiasm for pupil consultation are necessarily cautious. This is because it is not possible to know in advance what the consequences will be of injecting strong pupil voices into a classroom teaching system that has evolved over two centuries without listening to such voices. Will such a change be manageable by teachers? Will it be in all pupils' interests? What will be involved in making such a system manageable and beneficial for all?

One thing about which there now seems to be little doubt is that, from an early age, young people are capable of insightful and constructive analysis of their experiences of learning in school (eg Soo Hoo, 1993; Nieto, 1994; Rudduck et al, 1996). However, as Rudduck et al (1996: 173) point out:

> *... the conditions of learning that prevail in the majority of secondary schools do not adequately take account of the maturity of young people, nor of the tensions and pressures that they experience as they struggle to reconcile the demands of their social and personal development with the development of their identities as learners.*

The possibility that if schools could attend more to pupils' views about their learning experiences and preferences this would lead to improvement in pupil achievement is supported by recent school improvement studies (Sammons et al, 1997; Gray et al, 1999). The research reported in this book was therefore planned in order to look more closely at some of the problems and the possibilities for schools in attending more to pupil views.

We report two research projects, both undertaken within the framework of the Consulting Pupils Network (coordinated by Jean Rudduck and supported by the ESRC's Teaching and Learning Research Programme). The two research projects were conceived from different standpoints, but they complement each other in addressing what we believe to be two of the central issues for teachers in consulting pupils about their teaching and learning. On one hand, classrooms are complex settings for teachers to manage in order to facilitate their pupils' learning. Can teachers, in addition to all the other things which they have learned to take into account, also fruitfully take account of the insights and suggestions of their diverse pupils? On the other hand, classrooms are complex social worlds in which pupils are asked not only to learn but also to live much of their young lives. How might the social dynamics of the classroom, where the interactions among 30 often very different young people and their teacher both reflect and shape their diverse identities and interests as learners, influence the task of consulting pupils and taking account of their perspectives?

The first project (conducted by Donald McIntyre and David Pedder) was, at one level, a very pragmatic one, aimed at finding out whether teachers would find the ideas gathered from pupil consultation sufficiently useful to be incorporated into their practice. At another level, the project was informed by theoretical understandings of the task of classroom teaching. Noting six features of the complexity of classroom life identified by Doyle (1986: 394-395) – multidimensionality, simultaneity, immediacy, unpredictability, publicness and history – McIntyre (2000: 3-4) has argued that the implications for teachers include the following:

- their choices are never simple
- they must monitor and regulate several different activities at once
- they have little time, in the main, to reflect before acting
- detailed long-term planning is counterproductive and even short-term plans need to be very flexible
- what they do on any occasion can have important future repercussions
- planning and decision-making needs to take account of a class's history.

Against this background, McIntyre (2000: 18) suggests that there may be a dilemma:

> *Arguments that secondary school students are not sufficiently treated as partners in their own learning are highly persuasive, both in terms of their rights to have their perspectives taken into account and also instrumentally in terms of their commitment to learning. The lack of control which students have over their own lives in institutions which would claim to be serving their interests can indeed be seen as quite remarkable. Within the context of classroom teaching, however, the task for the teacher of treating students as partners while continuing to take responsibility for classroom activities and outcomes cannot but be seen (at least initially) as adding to the complexity of the teacher's task.*

This project took as its starting point the idea that pupils would be able to provide teachers with high quality ideas about their teaching. We wanted to know whether particular teachers, when they were able to find out in some depth about their own pupils' reflections on learning experiences in their classrooms, would be willing and able to change their practices in ways that took serious account of these ideas. If they did so, would they and their pupils view these changes as improvements? And would teachers who had such experiences be persuaded and able to adopt pupil consultation as a normal integral part of their classroom practice?

The second project (directed by Madeleine Arnot and Diane Reay) also involved researchers interviewing pupils, but here the focus was different. The interviews were aimed at finding out what pupils could tell us about the social world of the classroom. The emphasis was on the different conditions of learning experienced by different groups of pupils. How was the classroom experienced by girls and by boys, by working class and middle class pupils, by pupils of different ethnicities, and by pupils who had, up to this point, experienced different levels of academic success? In particular, the concern was with the social experiences in the classroom that shaped pupils' learning. How far were different groups of pupils able to talk to and be heard by teachers in what Bernstein (1996) refers to as 'the acoustic of the school'; how far had they developed confidence as classroom learners; to what extent did they feel included in the classroom as a learning community; and how much did they or others (including the teacher) feel they exercised control over classroom events? While the first project allowed for the possibility that different pupils might have different ideas about what helped their learning, this project explored the extent to which different groups of pupils had different things to say and whether consultation with different social groups could be valuable.

If we are serious about using pupil consultation to optimise teaching effectiveness, we need first to deepen our understanding of the social conditions of learning. Then we probably need to develop ways in which the different pupils in particular classrooms can be enabled to engage in dialogue with their teachers about how their particular contrasting social conditions help or hinder their learning. Our aim is that the two projects reported here should, between them, make a significant contribution to our understanding of the complexities and possibilities of pupil consultation for classroom teaching and learning.

2 The impact of pupil consultation on classroom practice

David Pedder and Donald McIntyre

The research project

We have little evidence of how teachers respond to pupil comments on teaching or how teachers use pupils' ideas to modify their practice. This project set out to explore these questions.

Teachers and pupils from six Year 8 classes (two each in English, Maths and Science) in three East Anglian schools were involved. We worked alongside teachers who were interested in contributing to research on consulting pupils.

The research was carried out in three stages between March 2000 and March 2001.

During the first stage, which consisted of five visits to each teacher and their pupils between March and May, the focus was on eliciting from pupils their ideas about classroom teaching and learning in the focal subject, and from the teachers their respective responses to their pupils' ideas. From each of the six classes, six fairly articulate pupils, three boys and three girls, were selected and invited to take part in individual interviews after observed lessons, three who were doing well and three who seemed neither to enjoy the subject nor to be doing well in it, 36 pupils in all. The project was explained to each of the classes and the six teachers each involved their classes in choosing the six pupils who would represent them. Interviews focused on what pupils judged to facilitate their learning in this teacher's class, what they regarded as unhelpful to their learning, and what alternative strategies and approaches their teacher might employ to the benefit of their pupils' learning. Throughout this first stage, teachers were increasingly asked to focus on planned changes in their practice in response to pupils' ideas and comments that they had read and judged to represent worthwhile and manageable innovations.

The second stage of the fieldwork took place over the remainder of the Summer term. Working with the same six teachers, interviews following observed lessons were held with the same six target pupils in order to elicit their judgements of teachers' modified classroom practice in the light of their ideas, and the ways in which the changes, as they perceived them, influenced their learning. Post-lesson interviews were also held with their teachers. These focused on their evaluations of the implementation of planned changes in the context of the observed lesson and the extent to which they judged the changes to have provided enhanced learning opportunities for their pupils.

A third stage of fieldwork was carried out during the following Autumn and Spring terms. All six teachers were interviewed with a view to discovering their perceptions of the sustainability and transferability to new classroom contexts of what they had learned from the previous year's experience. We wanted to find out if the six teachers continued to develop ways of learning about pupils' reactions to their teaching as part of their normal classroom practice and if they continued to use what they had learned to shape their teaching in different contexts.

Pupil suggestions for improvement

Pupils to varying degrees, but consistently, took advantage of the opportunities to provide ideas which they thought would enhance the quality of their learning. We found that some pupils could do this more articulately than others. For example, some were able to provide clear rationales and clear guidance about what it was they were asking for. Others, inexperienced in talking about their learning, struggled to find clarity and experienced difficulty putting their ideas into words. Some pupils, mainly the academically more successful pupils, demonstrated perspectives that signalled sympathetic understandings of classroom experiences in three distinct ways:

- First, they described their own private perspective: what helps and hinders their own personal learning.
- Second, they articulated a public perspective: a conscious understanding of the experiences of their classmates. These pupils clearly showed sympathy for the needs of their peers as well as themselves.
- Third, they demonstrated the capacity for taking the perspective of their teacher, particularly in accounts of decisions made by their teacher that went against their private learning preferences.

These more articulate pupils demonstrated an awareness of the complexities and dilemmas faced by classroom teachers to which researchers such as Doyle (1986) and McIntyre (2000) have drawn attention.

The researchers' questions

The researchers' questions were about what did, did not and might help the pupils' learning and the pupils' responses were to a remarkable degree focused on these matters. For example, we did not raise issues about the school curriculum; and in the pupils' responses, the curriculum context remained unchallenged. The concerns which pupils tended to emphasise centred on the mode of their engagement and the extent of their involvement within the established curriculum context of their classroom learning. The pupils tended to see the nature of their learning opportunities as overwhelmingly determined by their teachers, and so it was primarily their teachers' approaches and dispositions about which they spoke. But they concentrated, as asked, on how what the teachers did influenced their own learning opportunities. And although negative as well as positive things were said about the teachers' teaching, there was a quite striking absence of gratuitously personal, vindictive, trivial or silly comments. The task of contributing to the planning of their learning activities seemed to be accepted and undertaken by the pupils with the utmost seriousness.

Pupil consensus

One of our most striking findings was that there was a high degree of consensus among pupils, irrespective of teacher, subject, school, or the pupil's previous level of academic success, about what helped them to learn. Some were certainly more articulate than others, and of course the experiences that they reported varied across teachers, but the substance of their concerns was remarkably consistent. This consensus was apparent too across pupils' reports of what had and had not been helpful in observed lessons and their suggestions about alternatives that they would favour. In the remainder of this section, therefore, we shall not differentiate among categories of pupils, although we shall be quoting pupils drawn evenly from all the different groups involved. Similarly, we shall not discuss separately the approaches to teaching and learning that pupils found useful and those that they thought they would find useful. Our findings are such that we are able to concentrate on the central themes of what the pupils generally valued.

Four main categories of pupil comment were identified from pupils' accounts:

- engaging pupils more deeply in their learning
- contextualising learning more appropriately
- fostering a sense of agency and ownership among pupils
- arranging social contexts that are more amenable to learning.

Engaging pupils more deeply in their learning

Pupils made many suggestions that related to the depth of their engagement in classroom learning. They discussed deeper engagement in learning as involving thoughtful, motivated, purposeful and active participation. Guidance and support that pupils identified as particularly useful consisted of explanations in a language that is accessible to them:

> I think [the teacher] explained it very well. It was very easy ... she talks different from other teachers because she's like younger and she sounds more like us.

> When we first started doing Drama she helped us understand different acting techniques ... She explained it to us but in a way that we could understand.

Another pupil suggests certain modifications:

> It's simple language. Language that young kids would understand. You don't say, 'Oh we're doing an algebra test today'. You'd say, 'We're doing a missing number test today. Go and sit down and we'll hand out the papers. You've got to work out what the splat's covering, what numbers'... and kids would think it's better rather than algebra. I mean half the kids in my class don't even know what algebra is ... They'd understand it if you sat down, either explained it or did something fun with it.

However, pupils were quick to reject another teacher's adoption of an infantile tone:

> But with coordinates we draw line things and she was doing like little ski men down the slopes and things and going 'weeeeeeeee' and making us sound like we were six or something.

Pupils also wanted explanations that were concise:

> He is like extra sure on everything. He has to make sure that everyone's perfectly clear, so he goes through things and explains things clearly. But then that does take a long time ... and it sort of gets really boring.

> And she rambles on a bit and that makes us lose concentration ... she talks and talks and talks and talks and she doesn't stop. And that goes on for ages. We just get so bored that we lose concentration and start talking to our friends.

Explanations needed to be clear and to incorporate plenty of examples, to involve concrete demonstrations of new concepts and ideas, or to be supported by boardwork. These elements, of course, could be combined and in emphasising a varied approach, pupils were clearly sensitive, not only to their own learning preferences but also to differences among the preferences of their peers. Pupils were quick to point out the helpfulness to their learning of teachers they felt to be skilled in providing these kinds of support:

> I like the different things that she did in class. Like, with a stick and with doing it on the board and we were telling her and so it's just lots of different ways of showing you and trying to get it across ... Some people look at things different to other people. So some people might understand when she shows us with the pole and other people might not get that at all. And other people might understand it when she does it on the board so it's for the whole class to make sure that everyone understands.

> I think when it's done in a role play it's more ... it's not just kind of explained, it's kind of shown as well. So it's like every time someone says something, it's actually happening so it kind of goes together and makes a lot more sense that way.

Pupils also spoke about the importance of teachers asking questions as a way of sustaining deeper levels of active engagement among pupils:

> He just talks to himself and talks to us all and tells ... He asks very little questions. And I think that if he asked more questions then we'd become more alert instead of just sitting there like just listening to him all the time ... If he'd ask us more questions we would have to think a lot for the answers and stuff.

Some pupils wanted their teachers to distribute questions more fairly and to nominate individuals to respond. Other pupils argued the advantages of oral questioning over written work as a basis for teachers' assessment of their progress. What is striking about this pupil's account is her ability to take the perspective of her teacher. She balances the frustration she experiences at not being able to render a full account of her understanding through writing with the priorities of her teacher's assessment strategy as she perceives them:

> ... then we had to write it down, which kind of took loads of time, when we could've just remembered it. But I suppose she has to mark it and stuff so that's understandable, but it kind of took up some time and I'd rather just sort of acted it out or something ... She could just sort of pull people out of the group in turn and say, 'Well, what are we doing at the moment then? What are you doing now? What character are you playing? Do you understand the story OK? What's the story about?' So then she understands like directly with the pupil rather than just what they've written ... Because if you're writing it down then it takes longer, you kind of cut bits out that you don't think are very important; but they could actually be important for the teacher, you see. 'Cos you try and get it done so you can do the drama. But if you're talking to a teacher it would be quicker so you wouldn't feel you were rushed and you'd be able to say all your ideas out.

Some pupils spoke about the helpfulness of the kind of support from their teachers that encouraged them to think and to have the confidence to take their thinking further.

This pupil describes the importance of her Drama teacher's amplification and affirmation of her thinking as a powerful support and impetus for her further thoughtful engagement:

> *She helps you with your ideas. She helps you make your ideas matter if that makes sense ... It helps you know that somebody else knows your idea and they understand your idea and your idea isn't gobbledygook [laughs] ... because someone else says, 'That idea's really good, you should ...'. And then you think, 'Yeah, it's good. Someone else has told me it's good. I can go into that idea'. And if it didn't make sense she might say, 'I don't really understand that. Maybe you could explain it more to me.' And then I did.*

Through their suggestions for tasks that captured their imagination, pupils seemed to be calling for classroom learning to be driven by a different kind of dynamic: one that gave less prominence to the textbook or worksheets and the skills of reading and discursive note-taking and greater prominence to their own active involvement and decision-making.

However, some pupils told us about the kinds of writing activities that they found interesting. They emphasised their preference for graphic styles of writing such as spider diagrams, which pupils found helpful in thinking through connections among concepts, or posters, or tasks that combine writing with some form of drawing and colouring:

> *It was fun because everyone likes doing posters and everything. And then like you've got to draw and do stuff like that. I like that kind of thing. Like I like art and everything. So it's like if I don't always understand Maths, if you draw pictures and everything to help you get it, then it can help you to understand it more. So ... if you're enjoying something you're doing, then maybe you'll be more eager to do it more.*

Nevertheless, pupils were arguing that Drama lessons contained too much writing and not enough time devoted to acting and pupils in English were arguing for more opportunities to engage dramatically with texts. These kinds of changes, they argued, would lead to higher levels of motivated participation.

Ideas for a more active and practical engagement in learning tasks were important to pupils in other subjects too:

> We don't actually get to think for ourselves all the time when we're doing Science ... And I think it will be a little bit better if we actually do it ourselves more. ... And it's like when we're shown experiments as well, he shows us what happens instead of what we would like to find out ourselves ... But I thought that we could have done it ourselves if he'd just given us a little bit of help.

But learning tasks needed to have clear learning purposes. Pupils found that tasks that lacked a clear purpose were disengaging; they also needed to carry an adequate level of challenge.

Contextualising learning more appropriately

Pupils told us that work became more appropriately contextualised if there were evident connections between the task at hand and their current knowledge and understanding. The connections that pupils seemed to find helpful were sometimes achieved through their teacher's introduction of materials, objects and images that were already familiar to them. Connections were also made through teachers' incorporation in tasks of familiar images and genres. Where tasks were contextualised in these ways, pupils reported that they led to powerfully memorable and meaningful learning experiences:

> We've been learning more about coordinates and graphs and pictures and before Easter we learned about 'squeggs' ... it was an Easter egg - a square Easter egg. So it's an egg that's square. So it's 'squegg'. So we learned about sides of a 'squegg' and how many 'squeggs' we can get. And anybody that actually finished that work they got a 'squegg'. So that was fun. That was before Easter so that was novel.

> What might be nice to like try out? ... I think modernising an old story or something like that. Like a fairy tale or something like that and making it more modern ... Not having like, you know, perfect and pretty like it is in the fairy tale ... and then you put in some of the realistic things into it like poorer people and things like that and not necessarily, you know, like all 'goodies' are always rich and beautiful and all

the 'baddies' are like poor and low and ugly, you know ... But sometimes the hero could be like a homeless person and you know, those sorts of situations.

Contextualising learning appropriately also involved designing and using tasks that authentically resonate with pupils' wider concerns, experiences and aspirations inside and outside the school gate and beyond their learning careers at school. In this respect, pupils mentioned the vocational relevance of different learning experiences as helpful.

Pupils also told us about learning experiences that involved clear connections between the tasks they were asked to work with in the classroom and their social and interpersonal concerns outside it:

Drugs and alcohol, smoking and bullying. I think that's it ... We could produce a play like the whole class involved but like the whole of the class has a role in it ... People would perhaps pay more attention and, like, I can't say it but they'd like work more at it. They would be feeling how people ... how you would feel if you were a bully; how you would feel if you were trapped in the middle; how you would feel in certain situations. They would be able to like understand other people's feelings better.

Pupils seemed to be telling their teachers in concrete ways and with clear examples how the authenticity of their learning experiences could be enhanced by bringing tasks into closer alignment with the mental and social worlds that they inhabit both inside and outside the classroom.

Fostering a stronger sense of agency and ownership

Pupils spoke about agency and ownership in terms of opportunities for developing greater independence and autonomy in their classroom learning. They wanted to be trusted to learn:

It's nice to have a teacher who trusts you to do something on your own.

... usually some teachers really do not trust us to go outside on our own without a teacher. Our teacher let us go outside on our own in pairs.

The clear message from pupils was that they wanted to learn by doing more and taking more responsibility for themselves:

> Today in the lesson we was doing our own experiment on how many times a pin lands on its top end facing upwards and how many times it landed on the side. And then after that we put it into a graph ... It was pretty good because we hardly ever get to work alone and with our friends and stuff. And today we got to work on our own and not with the teacher's help or anything.

Pupils were prepared to create learning opportunities for themselves even where such opportunities fell beyond the planned expectations of their teacher – as in this Science lesson:

> ... we were just like packing away and so we just talked to each other about how much, like people on that table, we talked about how much theirs went down and stuff ... He didn't tell us. He just told us to pack away ... it was quite interesting 'cos you would ask them how long they burned theirs for and if the time would make a difference or something. And so it was quite interesting.

Yet some pupils spoke positively about the need to balance independent learning opportunities with more controlled opportunities:

> It's just sometimes you need the teacher and sometimes you don't really. It was just good to be like working with your friends, doing your own work ... Like at the beginning of the lesson ... she's got to tell you stuff and [you] use her to help you through it if you're stuck on something. But if you're like doing an experiment that you've made up by yourself, you don't need a teacher at all. Because you've made it up yourself and it's your work.

Some pupils spoke about the value of such independent learning opportunities as an important preparation for a sustained process of lifelong learning:

> If you're working on your own, everything is on you and you become more independent. So maybe working on your own for some experiments would be a good idea ... 'cos you don't stop learning at school. You'll learn things throughout your life so

if you have some independence after school you won't have a teacher to teach you things so you'll ... I think you'll be able to find out more things for yourself and things like that. Be able to ask yourself questions and be able to answer them. Things like that.

Others saw independence in their learning as a signal of their growing maturity – a key development in pupils' careers in the early years of secondary school:

We don't get that much homework and so we don't really think about Science that much ... We just like enjoying writing stuff that we found out ourselves ... It's like, like really sort of grown-up writing because you have to find information, take notes, then copy it all up and I think that's good.

For another pupil, being able to manage greater independence, and the sense of agency and ownership it offers, would help to encourage a readiness to reflect and think more deeply about her learning experiences:

... we should have written the conclusion ourself I think 'cos then we can think of what we'd actually learned instead of him telling us what we were meant to learn from it ... So it makes us think of what we have actually learned, so it makes us realise basically what the lesson was all about. If we had to do it ourself I think it sticks more in your mind because it's like your experience instead of someone else just doing it for you ...

Acquiring greater responsibility in their learning was strongly connected by some pupils to their sense of growing maturity and they experienced frustration at being denied opportunities to ask questions and make decisions:

This is just like children's work ... because they are telling us what to do and if we could think on our own what to do instead of having to be told the questions to ask ... and we could set it out how we want instead of having to do pie charts and stuff like that.

This pupil's rationale for wanting greater autonomy in classroom learning was articulated by her raw and fervent wish not merely to learn but to demonstrate that she has learned:

> *I really want to learn, but I want to show that I have learned, not just listen all the time. Like show that I've learned by doing things myself.*

Arranging social contexts more amenable to learning

Effective social contexts for learning were those that allowed pupils to collaborate with their peers. They described a number of different configurations in which such collaboration might be achieved. Foremost among the benefits that pupils identified was the scope provided by such arrangements to express themselves, to negotiate meanings and to develop understandings interactively through the medium of their classroom talk.

The awareness they demonstrated of a range of useful skills for responding and interacting with the ideas of peers is a striking feature of some accounts:

> *It's good because people can express their ideas. They can say what they think. They can tell people what they think instead of bottling up inside of them what they think. They can let out what they think of their ideas, what they think of other people's ideas. Like if someone's had an idea you can say, 'I don't really think that'll go', or, 'That'll be really good to what we're doing', and when you tell people that, they can say what they think and it just helps you. So ... if you know that their idea is better than yours then you'd have to say, 'Yeah, I think your idea is better than mine'.*

The formation of groups was of particular importance to pupils. Pupils did not report working in ability groups in class as a benefit. Beyond this, however, there was no clear agreement among pupils about which group formation they regarded as optimal. Some pupils reported the benefits of working in friendship groups, others reported the benefits of working in non-friendship groups:

> *... we adapt to different groups and come together with different groups and people, and the fact that she puts us with people that we don't usually work with is quite good ... I think sometimes people work with their friends and it*

doesn't work out so well ... but today it was people we don't usually work with. It was a different scene, different people and everybody had different ideas and putting all the ideas together came together really well.

However, forming groups composed of pupils who share the same motivation and desire to learn is difficult. Pupils reported their sense of frustration when grouped with peers who did not share the same level of interest:

... it was a bit hard because there were some people that wouldn't cooperate, and I think we could've chosen more people that we wanted to be with because there are some people that don't really pay attention as much as others and they mess about and you can't get anything done.

Some pupils suggested creating new opportunities for cross-age collaboration beyond the boundaries of year groups. For instance, a Maths teacher involved her Year 8 pupils in preparing posters that presented coordinates to their peers in Year 7. Pupils reported that providing exemplars of mastery in this way is motivating and helpful for their younger peers and an effective way for older pupils to consolidate their own understandings:

Well, like, the teacher just told us, like we tried to explain the basics of coordinates and everything ... we were trying to get it across to them as well ... So like it's sort of remembering what she'd told us and like telling other people about it. So telling them what she told us ... It helps us remember what she said ... because you have to have it clear before you tell other people ... we're going over it more in our heads ... and it helps them as well because like if they think, 'Well, children like around our age have done it, we can do it as well'. So they can see what we've done and everything ... Year 8s will know what they're [Year 7s] going to be thinking and everything, like 'I don't really understand anything'. So they can just put it clearly what they've been told.

Another pupil suggested opportunities for being able to present scientific understandings that his class had developed to pupils in other year groups as a useful preview and preparation for the next stages in their learning. He argued that assembly rather than the classroom lesson might be the more appropriate setting for such collaborations. The same pupil also suggested presentations by pupils between classes in the same year group as an opportunity to extend current understandings of a particular topic. And another pupil recommended opportunities to perform plays to pupils in different year groups as an opportunity to extend dramatic skills and techniques:

> ... we could also look at other people's plays ... If they performed to us one day that might expand our ideas ... maybe from the same year group or maybe the higher year group because they are learning different stuff from us and we could learn what they are doing as well ... Through their plays they will be doing their techniques that they learned in that year. Well, we could learn them by their plays, what they were doing in their plays and we could get a rough idea what that was.

In their accounts, pupils articulated a formidable range of ideas which clearly demonstrate their status as knowledgeable participants in the life of classrooms. Yet we wanted to know how the six teachers would respond to the range and quality of ideas in the transcripts of their pupils' accounts. It is to the responses of their teachers that we turn in the next section.

Teachers' responses to pupils' ideas

Transcripts of the interviews with each of the pupils were given to the teachers concerned within a week of the lesson, and the teachers were then interviewed about their initial responses to the pupils' ideas. Each of the six teachers was given three successive sets of transcripts and interviewed each time about their responses.

General reactions

In general, the teachers' overall reactions to their pupils' comments were very positive, although they did vary, both in the degree of their enthusiasm and in what they focused on. Least impressed were the two teachers who talked of 'no surprises', one of them indicating that the pupils had concentrated mainly on weaknesses in her teaching of which she was already aware. The other four teachers all found things to be surprised and pleased about. One was 'pleased that most of my pupils felt positive about [my subject] ... surprised they were as positive as they were'. A second was 'quite pleasantly surprised that there was a lot of common feelings coming through ... they seem to be reasonably consistent, a lot of these comments'. A third commented on the 'very mature approach' adopted by the pupils: 'They seem to be reflecting not only on their own learning style but on the learning style of other pupils in the class'.

All of the teachers found that their pupils were offering them plenty of constructive and sensible ideas that they could use. They found most of the ideas to be 'pretty fair'; and they generally thought that, as one put it, the pupils 'were generally, in a very polite, nice way, good at criticising the lessons'. At best, the pupils' ideas were 'exciting' and 'creative'. Accordingly, the teachers were generally very receptive to pupils' suggestions.

Appraising pupil ideas

It was clear, however, that the teachers examined pupil comments and suggestions very critically before deciding to act on them. Ideas were appraised in terms of their inherent merits but also often in terms of their source.

Sources of ideas

Although the interviews were anonymous, the pupils generally made no efforts to disguise their identities and the teachers correspondingly had little difficulty in working out who was saying what. This was important to all the teachers, primarily because they wanted to know how representative the views expressed were. Thus they were usually much more interested when suggestions of similar sorts came from several pupils. Their reflections on what they considered the most important ideas from pupils are full of phrases such as 'A lot of pupils mentioned ...', 'Quite a few suggested ...', 'More than one of them said it', 'A lot of them said ...'.

Numbers, however, were not enough. It was also important that well-supported suggestions should be attractive for all the class:

> I think that the pupils who are making the suggestions are ones that see themselves as good at drama, who perhaps assume that they will get a big role.

> You see, I know who that is ... it wouldn't work well with the whole class, I'd lose too many of the class.

Sometimes, therefore, interesting ideas were discarded because the teacher could not see how they could be used effectively for everybody. Sometimes, teachers accepted the diversity of views as an indication that there was no need to change:

> One was slightly critical about doing this thing too long ... there were others who said they'd rather it went on a bit longer. So looking at that, if they're the two extremes, then perhaps I did get the balance right.

In other cases, however, teachers struggled to work out how to meet the needs of different groups of pupils, as in the following case where a teacher was a little shocked to learn that several of his pupils found him somewhat loquacious:

> And there was almost a complaint actually that I kind of over-explained it at that point. But I've also had comments from some pupils that they actually like me to explain things well ... you know, I don't think that's something I should stop doing, but perhaps try to be a little bit less verbose about it ... something to watch for really, that's all.

The teachers' primary concern in attending to the specific sources of ideas was with ensuring that the consultation enhanced the classroom learning experiences of all their pupils, and that it did not lead to some being disadvantaged. They were also however alert to the fact that some pupils seemed especially thoughtful and creative in their suggestions, and they evoked comments such as 'She could do all my plans!'

Criteria for judging pupil ideas

Pupil ideas seemed to be subjected by teachers to severe examination on a range of criteria. Teachers were at their most severe when they doubted the validity of pupils' accounts of classroom reality:

> I disagreed with what she said. She said that there were about four titles (to choose from). There were loads, about 15. I think she had enough choice there, I really do.

> *They say they don't want so much homework. They give the impression, one or two of them, that they do homework every night but we only have it once a week.*

Practicality was the criterion most often used explicitly by teachers in judging pupil suggestions: 'Could we actually do this?' They make it clear that they have to operate in a very constrained way. The National Curriculum imposes one direct kind of constraint while the related testing regime severely constrains the timetabled time available:

> *[The suggestion of open-ended group projects]: I'm always thinking I've only got three weeks to get through the content before they're assessed. It's a different type of learning and they will remember an awful lot more from what they've presented and because they're proud to achieve, but again it's weighing up whether the time spent on that is going to be useful when they've got all these hurdles to jump over.*

Among the other practical constraints which made it difficult for teachers to be more responsive to their pupils' ideas were those of teachers' own time, equipment, space and, especially, specialist space:

> *[Using drama to support English lessons] is a good idea but would involve me collaborating with another teacher, because I'm not teaching the Shakespeare, which would be possible, but ...*

> *They would like to be given the opportunity to work in pairs and sometimes even on their own, which is something we probably don't do too much due to shortages of equipment really.*

Teachers very commonly saw their pupils' ideas as being very sensible in principle but not possible in practice.

Teachers might also decide that their pupils were wrong in principle, that what they were suggesting was not educationally desirable:

> *I'm very much against it in actual fact, organising in ability groups.*

Another pupil made the comment that they thought it would be useful to learn from their mistakes in planning and carrying out the experiments. The teacher responded:

> That's one comment I do disagree with really ... I can't see the point in having them plan an experiment if it's not really up to standard or if it's basically wrong.

Selecting pupil suggestions for use

The teachers were invited to select suggestions from their pupils which they could incorporate into their practice and in general they had little difficulty. The easiest suggestions for teachers to accept were of course those which encouraged them to do more of the good things they already did, and there were plenty of suggestions of that kind:

> Everybody liked the role playing. So I'll try and include that. I've always done that, so that's something I'll try and maintain.

> The idea that being given more space, kind of literal space, you know, go down the corridor and work, one of them said that that really helped them ... and I did notice that they worked better when they were all spread out separately.

> I think the strongest point that came out was the idea of trust, the fact that I'd allowed them to go off around the school in pairs or threes to collect their own leaves in the sites they chose. They all seemed very pleased with the idea they'd been trusted to do that ... and it had some impact on how one or two of them have worked.

The other most easily accepted suggestions were of things that the pupils remembered having done on previous occasions with that teacher. Sometimes these suggestions were made in comparative terms, the previous approach being said to be preferable to what had been done in a recent lesson. The teachers seemed to value such feedback and, in some cases, to concur. In other cases, the pupils seemed simply to be telling the teacher, either explicitly or implicitly, about how valuable or enjoyable the remembered activity had been:

> *There was the bit about feedback that they felt that they needed more time ... going back into a circle ... and I think that suggestion, thinking of that other lesson, would have been much better, actually ... they seemed to quite value finding out what other people were doing ... more than I imagined they would do really. So, spending more time on the feedback ... yes, in the circle.*

> *It's a technique I've used before but having read it reminded me that that would be a good start for them, to give them that chance to interact ...*

The pupils were also ready to identify weaknesses of specific lessons or of the individual teachers, and the teachers were often ready to accept these judgements:

> *I talk too much. I agree with them, generally ... But it does depend on the circumstances.*

> *I think I was quite aware of what was wrong about that particular lesson - rather boring way to introduce a six-week project to read out that part of the story, so I wouldn't repeat that exercise of reading it.*

While many of the pupils' suggestions came directly from what they did or did not value in their teachers' practices, there were many suggestions too that depended on new ideas that the pupils themselves had developed. Quite often teachers welcomed these ideas as sensible and as entirely consistent with their own thinking. Some suggestions, for example, were related by the teachers to things that they had done with other classes:

> *I like the idea of this fairy story suggestion which funnily enough I had done with another group ... it would be completely new for them and it would be quite a nice focus.*

> *That was one of the ideas I thought I could use - to have individual extension exercises available for one or two ... It's something I used to do when we had a more individualised scheme really. It's bringing back the old ideas.*

Other suggestions were welcomed simply as good ideas, perhaps ideas which the teachers would have thought of if they had had more time:

> Other suggestions included 'cut the story and use more of an outline' and that definitely was a good idea; and I think personally, as a teacher, I should have thought more to make that introduction punchier, livelier, more dramatic.

> I think one thing that came out was they'd like to discuss wrong results more, which I think is a fair comment really ... perhaps I'll try to make an effort to at least do one piece of investigational work where we spend a lot of time evaluating it and so forth.

It was frequently noticeable that the teachers, when faced with new ideas that they found interesting, would not simply accept or reject these ideas, but would instead develop them. Frequently, they would make connections between rather different things that different pupils had said. Often they would take a specific idea offered by a pupil and develop it into a much more general strategy for use in diverse circumstances. Very commonly, they would adapt the idea to produce one which better fitted their own purposes. The following are just two examples of teachers' active development of pupil ideas:

> She said: 'I'd like to do it as a newspaper article ... it's like real life and it's more grown-up instead of having to do this, like children's work.' So it seems to make it more valuable, I think, giving a context within a real-life situation ... maybe, say, you're writing a story for such-and-such an age-group, and then get them to go to a school and read the stories to them ... a greater purpose than just writing stories.

> They were referring to enjoying doing the poster work and presenting information in pictorial form. And they found that easy to remember. They preferred revising things like that, which actually makes a lot of sense. So I suppose the key issue from a teaching point of view is how much quality information they're getting down ... I think that would probably need fairly specific guidelines. Or possibly even, it's set me thinking, I would often do a spider diagram with them for revision, because it's quite clear and pointedly factual. But possibly I could give them a spider diagram and get them to translate that into a poster, something they would be keen to refer back to.

As has been indicated, the teachers found it relatively easy to assimilate many of their pupils' suggestions to their repertoires for future work. They also rejected quite a lot of ideas because of their impracticality or for other reasons. But between these two large categories there were some ideas which were in diverse ways more problematic for the teachers:

- In one or two cases, teachers reported that they had been persuaded simply to **change their minds** by the evidence of their pupils' experiences and arguments. The unhappiness and frustrations of one of her pupils persuaded one teacher that it was after all sensible to allow pupils sometimes to work in friendship groups. Another was persuaded that her practice of encouraging pupils who had been absent simply to 'slot in' to the ongoing activity wasn't good enough and would have to be changed.

- One teacher confessed that a pupil's pleas had convinced him that the time had come for him to **get round to innovating** through the use of new electronic equipment. 'I haven't been using it because it isn't part of me yet', he said, 'but they've seen it, they know about it, there's no reason why they can't use it ... it's something which perhaps I should try and incorporate routinely ...'

- Some of the teachers, while not ready to commit themselves to any new course of action by particular pupil comments, were stimulated by these comments to engage in **serious reflection**. One, for example, on learning that some pupils had found it 'babyish' when she had given them wooden cubes to make mathematical work more practical, reflected on the likelihood that not all of them would need such support and on how she could in future most effectively offer pupils choices in such circumstances. Another, on learning that pupils were asking for more difficult ideas, reflected on how that could most appropriately be managed.

- Sometimes, the teachers were not persuaded of the practicality or the likely effectiveness of pupil suggestions. In several cases their reaction to this, however, was not rejection of the idea but rather '**It's questionable, let's try it**'. A Drama teacher, for example, faced with the suggestion that she should cast herself in the director role and give all the pupils different acting or other roles, had visions of 'being spread too thinly' and of the chaos that might develop, but decided to discuss it with the class and 'if they opt for that, even if it's a disaster, it's a learning experience for them and it's a learning experience for me. That's how to change things really'. A somewhat more extreme version of this was the response of one teacher to several different suggestions – a response which might be described as **reluctant compliance**. While seeing the strength of the pupils' arguments, she tended to articulate several reasons for not accepting the suggestions and concluded 'I'm not happy with it but I'm going to have a go at it anyway'. It seemed that, although she did not find the pupil arguments convincing, she felt bound to take account of the seriousness with which the suggestions were formulated.

Teachers' use of pupils' ideas

After reflecting on the pupil ideas in the transcribed interviews, each teacher drew up a list of pupil suggestions to implement over the next six weeks or so. The second phase of the research focused on what happened when the teachers tried to put these ideas into practice. In this section we shall first consider the success of these efforts and then look at the longer-term impact which the consultation project had on the teachers' practices.

We were able, in the previous two sections, to generalise across the six classrooms, both about the pupils' ideas and about the teachers' responses to them. We do not find that possible, however, in this section. The teachers differed quite widely both in what they did and also in the outcomes of their efforts. Our report of this second stage of the research, therefore, is organised in terms of short stories of what happened with different teachers.

Pupil ideas that teachers made to work

We start with a number of brief accounts of teachers' largely successful use of pupil ideas.

Catharine and 'The Lady of Shalott'

Catharine is a young English teacher. During the first phase of the research she had identified a substantial list of pupil ideas which she wished to incorporate into her teaching. While a good many of these ideas were building on existing strengths of her teaching and on things that she had done before, others derived from negative evaluations of her teaching or were ideas about which she was not totally convinced but was ready to try.

For the final half-term of the school year, Catharine planned a unit on Tennyson's 'The Lady of Shalott' and carefully built into the successive lessons of this unit the various pupil ideas that she had decided to use. She told the class that she had read the interview transcripts and would be using some ideas from them, but did not identify either the specific ideas or the specific sources from which they had come.

In the first two lessons, about the setting of the poem and about imagery, Catharine aimed to be much more specific about the aim and purpose of the lesson, to have less teacher talk, to use peer explanations, to nominate non-volunteers to answer her questions and especially to be more practical. By her own account and those of the interviewed pupils, all of these were effectively achieved. As one pupil reported:

> I like the way we went about the lesson: we had to draw what we thought was there and I like drawing. If it's turned into something people enjoy, then you learn it easier ... I understood the lesson and I understood what was being said and I understood the task and I did it.

The next observed lesson, responding to a pupil suggestion for more simulation work, involved the pupils acting as knights investigating the lady's death and key 'witnesses' from the poem. Catharine was pleased with how the pupils took on their roles and stayed in character; they showed themselves to be greatly intrigued as to what had happened and very eager to ask significant questions and to generate theories on the basis of the evidence gathered. The lesson was experienced as different, enjoyable and useful because 'it was basically like a game and we had to figure out what had happened and like ask questions to find out'.

A later lesson sought to explore the wider fantasy world in which the poem was set. For homework, the pupils had been asked to find out stories of King Arthur and now groups were asked to prepare presentations of these stories. Here, in accordance with the pupil ideas, the groups were deliberately constructed as non-friendship groups, no clear dividing line was maintained between

'English' and 'Drama', pupils were given more space, literally and metaphorically, the teacher talked less and the work was more 'practical'. Catharine commented:

> In the past I've not given them so much freedom and I think the way they did it today was actually more interesting for them ... They probably learned more from it 'cos they probably listened more and they were more interested in doing it in the first place ... I think they worked better like that because they'd got their own space.

Here then we have an example of a teacher who was willing to make a considerable effort not only to listen carefully to her pupils' ideas but also to respond to their suggestions very creatively and thoughtfully. Her careful choice and interpretation of the suggestions seemed to ensure their practicality and that they all contributed to teaching and learning that both she and her pupils judged to be highly successful.

Laura and 'very fun' Mathematics

Laura is an experienced Mathematics teacher and Head of her Mathematics department. She was pleased to learn from the interviews that most of the pupils seemed positive about Mathematics and about her Mathematics teaching, and she was struck by the care and thought that they put into responding to the interviews. From the pupil suggestions, she planned to incorporate in her teaching more difficult problems as extension work, to use computer facilities more, to have more competitive games, and to increase opportunities for pupils to share their ideas with each other.

Laura didn't say anything to pupils about her intention to make use of their ideas. In the first lesson in which she intended to do so, the planned use of ICT and of planned interactive pair work was 'sabotaged' by technical problems of access to the Internet. The following weeks were occupied mainly with examinations, but during that time Laura managed to implement one of the pupil suggestions, for paired work in revising. Laura judged that it had been more effective than her usual practice because pupils could give more time, with less distraction and more sustained attention to the task. 'It was a pretty good lesson actually ... I was surprised by how much we got done'. The class's test results for that unit were better than were to be expected from previous performance and from earlier informal assessment during that module. She was persuaded that the idea was 'really good' and was delighted 'that it was a pupil's idea in the first place'.

In the next lesson in the IT room, things went much more smoothly than previously. However, Laura found that the pupils' ICT knowledge wasn't as good as expected so that the basic tasks took much longer and the planned extension work was less used than intended. Laura persisted, however, and in a further lesson in the IT room was again pleased by the way the pupils settled into the task, and she was now able to build on previous work done by the pupils both in Maths and in ICT classes. 'They were all fully focused most of the time ... clearly [using ICT effectively] does make a big difference'. Because of pupil views, Laura had reworked a probability module to do this lesson on the computers and to build in a strong competitive game element. Using ICT also 'forced' the opportunity for pupils to work together and to learn from talking to each other.

Among the things clearly exemplified by Laura's story are the considerable practical and organisational difficulties which can face a teacher who attempts to make use of pupil ideas. Indeed, the events outlined above seem to have been merely the tip of the iceberg: when asked 'Are there any other pupils' ideas that you have incorporated over the last five weeks?', Laura's response was 'Not really. I mean I've tried to but they haven't worked or I haven't had time to do it properly, or the people who it would be best for didn't get it finished'.

Nonetheless, Laura remained highly enthusiastic about the experience. The project, she said, had encouraged and reinforced her use of 'very fun' activities that are both enjoyable and cater for visual and spatial and active learning styles:

> You often question such things, especially if they end up being totally disorganised in your view ... but these interviews gave me a chance to listen and hear that they were getting something out of it ... I've found it surprisingly useful, much more useful than I expected it to be.

Richard and going deep into pollution

Richard is a Science teacher who was in his first year in the school. He was working with a 'top' Year 8 set. While he found the ideas in the interview transcripts generally consistent with his own thinking about Science and how it should be learned, he was also uncertain about the practicality of many of the suggestions made. Nevertheless, he identified a long list of ideas which he thought it would be possible and useful to implement.

Richard's first follow-up lesson provided a very clear example of unsuccessful implementation of pupils' ideas. It was fairly clear too why it was unsuccessful. Richard had not been persuaded of the merits of the idea, he had used the idea in an inappropriate context and, by his own admission, he had not planned for its use at all well. Fortunately, he then went on to implement other pupil suggestions much more successfully.

A lesson observed by the researcher two weeks later was the third in a series on pollution. Richard had planned the series to embody pupil suggestions for less teacher explanation, more independence for pupils in conducting their work, more inductive experiments, more time to evaluate the results of experiments and within-class presentations by pupils. The pupils had spent two double periods doing some small experiments of their choice, and exploring issues on the Internet and in the library. In this lesson some of them had to present their findings, with posters and talk. Richard commented that 'very good quality research was done, reporting on a range of different kinds of pollution ... quite complicated, in-depth stuff'. He judged that there were no real disadvantages in pupils studying in this way, in accordance with their suggestions, and they were clearly motivated, collaborating, attentive to each other's presentations, and having fun doing it. 'They'll remember it better ... One or two of them thought about things that I hadn't thought about ... they've had opportunities to think deeply that we don't normally give them ... It is a little more time-consuming.' Richard had not told the pupils he was acting on their ideas, but pupil interviews clearly showed that they realised that he was doing so, and they too were in no doubt about the advantages, both for their motivation and for the quality of their learning, of the approach adopted.

Successful implementation of pupil ideas is not then a matter of some teachers having a distinctive gift or style. Richard was not only very diffident generally about accepting and using pupil ideas, he was also quite spectacularly unsuccessful when he made his first attempt at doing so. But then, by using a number of pupil ideas intelligently and carefully, he masterminded a project which in their opinion and in his own was equally spectacularly successful.

Pupil ideas that didn't work

We have highlighted above the successes that three teachers experienced in implementing their pupils' ideas. Along the way, we noted some of the less successful efforts of two of them. Now we focus on some perhaps more profound problems experienced by two of the other teachers who worked with us.

Jane's ambitious plans

Jane is an English and Drama teacher and her consultation work for the research project was with a Drama class that she met once a week. She was one of the teachers who in the first phase was particularly impressed by the pupils' comments and most responsive to them. She found herself in sympathy with many of the suggestions they made and reported herself as changing her mind about some aspects of her teaching in the light of pupil ideas.

On the basis of her reading of the transcripts, Jane identified a number of pupil suggestions which she wanted to follow up in her teaching in the final half-term of the year. Her first step in implementing these suggestions was to bring together the five 'pupil representatives' who had been selected by the pupils the previous term as those who would be interviewed by the researcher. As Jane saw it, it was important to integrate the pursuit of these ideas with substantial delegation of decision-making to the class, starting with whole-class consultation. Jane delegated most of the planning and conduct of this whole-class consultation exercise to the class representatives. Consideration of the diverse ideas which had been generated was integrated into a task of choosing topics for, and an overall approach to, the drama work for the next few weeks. A central part of the decision-making was to be discussions in groups, with the class representatives deciding the groups' membership and themselves leading the groups. Unfortunately, as was to emerge, Jane had underestimated the underlying tensions: the basis on which classroom groups should be formed was a very important matter for the pupils and the elected representatives were increasingly being seen by their peers as a little elite.

'So', Jane reported after the whole-class consultation, 'it all seemed to be going swimmingly and they were so enthusiastic when we arrived this morning ... they all seemed very confident ... and then they came in and it was ... it was somehow a bit negative from word go ...'. The composition of the groups was, it seemed, the first major contentious issue. The tasks that the groups were given also seemed to lead to friction. Then, as planned, the whole class came together again in a circle, the five representatives each reported their group's conclusions, and there was an open discussion of the various ideas and how the preferred ideas should be carried forward. 'Everybody had ideas', a pupil reported but, Jane noted, 'it was very very difficult to get them to listen to each other ... I have never known such hostility really within a group'. The antagonisms culminated in two of the class representatives, as a third explained, 'getting a bit upset at the end because I don't think they felt they were being listened to ... and they just sort of stormed out ...'.

Although the class had made some decisions about how to move forward, Jane was subsequently absent through illness and, when she returned, decided that it would be 'virtually impossible' to pursue what had been decided in the very limited time available before the end of term. She did, however, for the remaining work of that term, respond to the central idea expressed in the whole-class consultation, that of allowing pupils to work in friendship groups of their own choice.

With hindsight, it seems to us that, while rightly impressed by the insights which the pupils had offered, Jane probably exaggerated their capacity to plan and to manage the activities of the classroom. In her proper eagerness to engage all the pupils in planning their own learning activities, she underestimated the complexity of the planning and management tasks which she was delegating to some of them. There are, we believe, important lessons to be learned from Jane's experience. However keen we may be to share classroom decision-making with pupils, we can only do so effectively in so far as they have had adequate opportunities to develop the necessary expertise. We can safely ask pupils to share their ideas with us and then make maximum use of their ideas in our own decision-making. We have to be more cautious, however, in asking them to share our teaching responsibilities.

Lorna's struggles with the complexities of teaching

Lorna is a Mathematics teacher, in her first year at the school in which she was teaching. She seemed to be quite defensive in her interpretation of pupil suggestions: 'They've picked up weaknesses I am already aware of', she said. While she accepted most things the pupils said as having some merit, she also viewed them as telling only half the story. Lorna emphasised that everything was a matter of judgement, with a balance having to be achieved among the various needs of the pupils, various teaching purposes, and practical concerns, so whatever the pupils said had to be balanced against other considerations.

Nonetheless, Lorna did commit herself to making changes and, in the second stage of the research, told the pupils that there were going to be changes in the light of their comments: less talk from her, more activity-based work, more discussion, more use of peer explanation, and more open-ended tasks.

The first observed follow-up lesson, for example, was devoted to an open-ended problem-solving task. The pupils tended to be fairly positive about the task: 'It wasn't that boring 'cos I was actually concentrating and working really hard'. Lorna was pleased to see some groups engaged in effective collaborative problem-solving, although several other groups had needed suggestions from her. 'On the whole, it did work', she said, but went on to express disappointment about the noise level, the limited extent of pupils' explanations of their solutions, pupils' lack of effort, their failure to accept the challenge, and therefore their lack of progress. She also expressed doubts about her own role: 'I don't know whether I led them too much'. She wouldn't really be able to know until the test, she said, whether this was more effective than her more usual approach; it was certainly more risky.

Lorna's doubts about whether her efforts to change had been of any value were not generally shared by her pupils. Although some said 'nothing's really changed', most made comments like:

> She's started to give us problems to do and you learn to work on your own with friends, which is good.
>
> She's asking you more often what your results are and how you did it and it helps just to see how the others did it.
>
> She's talking less and getting into activities more quickly, like this morning she didn't ramble on a lot about it.

Despite such generally positive responses, Lorna continued to be sceptical about the value of the pupils' suggestions and her own implementation of them. 'I've received more, I think, honest opinions about what students want from the lessons and so on', she said, 'I'm just not sure that I see there's something that I get from it … I don't think they've addressed the learning … it's perhaps not being able to distinguish what it is that they want to get out of their classroom activities'. She also thought that there were too many constraints, primarily the frequent assessment, which prevented her from being more imaginative in response to pupil suggestions for more experiential types of learning. In summary, Lorna concluded, 'I feel that the contributions the pupil ideas have made to my teaching have been limited and I've been disappointed that I haven't been able to do more'.

Thus it was clear that, whatever the pupils might think, the consultation exercise was not a success from Lorna's perspective and was not going to have a longer-term impact on her teaching. She left the school at the end of the year, and when she was visited in her new school in the following spring, she did not think that her teaching had been influenced in any way by the consultation project and she had not engaged in any consultation activities in the new school.

All the things that Lorna had to say about the complexity of teaching and about the constraints within which teachers have to work seem to us right. Her commitment in nonetheless making major efforts to implement pupil suggestions were highly laudable, as was the success which, in her pupils' eyes, she achieved. But pupil consultation did not work for her; and the key reason for that may be that for teachers to benefit from pupil consultation they must have a basic confidence that pupils do potentially have something significant to offer; and Lorna did not have such confidence.

Longer-term impacts of pupil consultation

We interviewed each of the teachers once more, between December and March in the following school year, about their reflections on the project and especially about how it had influenced them. Would the good ideas which they had in the previous summer sought to integrate into their teaching have a longer-term impact on their teaching? And would they have been sufficiently persuaded of the value of pupil consultation to incorporate consultation procedures into their own practice? We shall explore these two questions mainly through revisiting one of the teachers, Catharine, who had achieved considerable success in her earlier implementation of pupil ideas, and through introducing Matthew, the sixth teacher involved in the project.

Catharine and the National Curriculum

Even at the time of the impressive success of her 'Lady of Shalott' unit, Catharine was sober in her own assessment of its implications. The whole experience had, she thought, been very useful for her own professional development, but its implications for her future practice were not so clear:

> Of course, it's getting towards the end of year so it doesn't bother me as much now, but if this was earlier on in the year I would be worried that I would be neglecting basic literacy skills by doing all these things. At other times, I couldn't be quite so responsive; we need to balance it with learning all the specified skills, writing and comprehension.

(Richard made very similar comments about his successful pollution unit.)

When Catharine was interviewed in the following January, her views had not changed: 'I did find the interviews you did with the pupils really enlightening, and there are a couple of things that I've taken out of that as kind of personal targets'. However, she thought that most of the changes she had made when teaching the poetry unit in the summer had been specific to that unit. She didn't have a Year 8 group this year, 'but when I do teach poetry with my Year 7, I will use a much more practical approach ... because I think it worked well'. Overall, the consultation project was 'not radically changing the way I teach', although she was 'probably more aware of the benefits of such practical work after that project and perhaps more liable to use it with certain classes'. Also there were major curriculum and examination constraints, as she had suggested earlier, on the adoption of such a practical approach.

Catharine's thinking about consultation was quite similar: from the start she was uncertain about consultation procedures in future. Individual interviews were not practical because of time constraints. Instead of questionnaires, she favoured the idea of 'chatting' with classes: 'It's probably something we don't do enough as teachers.' By the time of the January interview, Catharine had conducted one such spontaneous consultation with a Year 10 class: 'Some of them were moaning and saying "Oh we're fed up, this is boring ...", so I said to them "OK, what can I do to make it more interesting for you?" and they responded: "More practical" and ... "More drama" ... and just before Christmas we did a bit ... it was partly, it was the last two weeks of term and I didn't want to do anything really serious'.

After the high quality responsiveness to pupil ideas apparent in her 'Lady of Shalott' unit, Catharine's readiness in the following year to take advantage of pupil consultation only around the margins of the 'really serious' work may be seen as quite disappointing. That someone as clearly able as Catharine did not do more may perhaps fairly reflect the need for teachers, in present circumstances, to have very considerable confidence, commitment and expertise if they are to engage effectively with pupil consultation in the context of 'really serious' work.

Matthew, a convert from scepticism

Matthew is a Science teacher, head of his Science department, who was working with one of the lower Year 8 sets. He initially seemed somewhat sceptical of the value of the consultation, commenting on the first set of transcripts: 'I don't think there are any great surprises in there for me ... in many ways what I would expect, such as pupils wanting to do more practical'. His fuller response combined a sympathy with the pupils' general perspective with a sustained scepticism about specific suggestions. For example, he questioned the common pupil view that they had to do too much writing and their belief that peer explanations helped their scientific understanding. But he considered the transcripts carefully and was very ready to try out and to evaluate a wide range of pupil suggestions. As the project developed through the first two stages, his enthusiasm seemed to grow and, despite disruptions, he tried out as many of the pupil ideas as possible.

At the end of the second stage, Matthew commented as follows:

> The opportunity to get some insights into pupils' thoughts about lessons has been fascinating ... you become aware that some of them have more positive attitudes towards their learning than is necessarily apparent in the classroom ... It's made me kind of ... aware that I've got into a routine way of working, and it isn't necessarily the routine that they would want. And then to be able to change that routine and see if it has had an effect; and that they do recognise that a change has taken place. Quite how that would have improved the quality of their learning is hard to evaluate ... certainly it's had an impact on their motivation ...

This enthusiasm was equally apparent when Matthew was visited in the following December. He was confident that his teaching had been significantly changed by the previous year's consultation:

> I've particularly made a point of getting as much practical work as possible into what I'm doing. And then within that, allowing pupils at times some choice in terms of which activity they are going to do.

Matthew had also been active in developing formal consultation procedures with his Year 8 class, through questionnaires followed up by whole class discussion:

> I'd like to think I could try to keep this going and perhaps extend it beyond this Year 8 group. I might look at disseminating it to the Science department through talking about it at a departmental meeting. 'It's worked for me, if you want to have a go, this is a model that we've used.' If I were selling it, it would be: 'When presented properly to pupils, it gives them a kind of sense of responsibility about their learning, and they respond very positively. And to get that feedback on how I'm working and the impact it's having is very useful, because it allows me to reflect in an informed way on my practice. And hopefully, it allows you to be a bit more effective at hitting the right buttons with the class ... '

At the beginning of the project Matthew was one of the more sceptical of the six teachers. By the following year, he was clearly carrying forward the idea of pupil consultation with enthusiasm and vigour, more than any of the other teachers. This clearly reflected his personal professionalism – his readiness to examine ideas critically and to try them out in his own practice. It is also worth noting, however, that the other teacher whose enthusiasm for pupil consultation grew throughout the project was Laura, the other head of department involved. Laura, it may be remembered, had been excited to discover that some of the more demanding teaching strategies which she favoured, but had been thinking of abandoning, were highly valued by her pupils. She was still excited by this when she was interviewed in the following December, and correspondingly committed to developing pupil consultation, despite all the time constraints that made it difficult. It seems possible that teachers need the expertise and confidence which these two heads of department clearly had if they are both to see the potential that pupil consultation has to offer and also to confront the difficulties involved in incorporating it into the already very complex work of classroom teaching.

Comment

Each of the stories we have told in this section has been different, so we have to be very cautious about reaching any general conclusions from them. We do however tentatively suggest that these stories support the following hypotheses:

- Teachers can make direct use of pupils' suggestions to plan teaching which is motivating for pupils and which seems likely to contribute usefully to their classroom learning.

- The effectiveness of teachers' use of pupils' suggestions depends on careful planning and may be undermined by the diverse contingencies which can influence the effectiveness of teaching.

- The effectiveness of teachers' use of pupils' suggestions depends on teachers not relying on undeveloped pupil capacities to plan or manage aspects of classroom life.

- The effectiveness of teachers' use of pupils' suggestions depends on teachers having a basic confidence in pupils' capacity to contribute usefully to thinking about how classroom teaching and learning can be improved.

- Under present circumstances, where teachers tend to feel themselves to be tightly constrained, many are likely to feel pressurised into limiting their use both of pupil consultation and of pupil ideas for classroom teaching and learning to marginal contexts, such as the last weeks of a term or a year.

- There are experienced, expert and confident teachers, especially perhaps heads of department, who are able to implement practically useful schemes of pupil consultation with their own classes, and to make effective use within the normal curriculum of the ideas they derive from such consultation.

Reflections and conclusions

In this project, we set out to explore teachers' responses to, and uses of, pupils' ideas about what their teachers could do that would most help their learning. We chose ways of consulting pupils which we hoped would enable them to make their suggestions as fully, thoughtfully and uninhibitedly as possible.

The suggestions which pupils made, although clearly related to their experiences in particular classrooms, showed strikingly common tendencies, irrespective of teacher, subject, school or pupils' previous academic success. The teaching approaches they suggested were designed to engage them more deeply, more actively, in more diverse ways, more sociably and with more responsibility in classroom learning activities. More academically successful pupils, while sharing the same emphases as others, tended to be more articulate in elaborating their ideas.

The teachers tended to be surprised by the richness, the positive nature, the insightfulness and the good sense of pupil ideas. They examined these ideas critically, especially in terms of their practicality; they also found that many of the ideas reflected elements of their own current or past practice and that still more of them echoed their own educational thinking. It was therefore not difficult for each of them to choose some pupil ideas that they knew they could confidently pursue; and some were also happy to try out ideas that were new to them.

Although some factors were identified which could prevent successful outcomes, the teachers showed that thoughtful and committed implementation of pupils' ideas can, both in the short- and the longer-terms, lead to classroom teaching of enhanced quality.

3 The social dynamics of classroom learning

Madeleine Arnot and Diane Reay

The research project

Our project focused on the social conditions of learning in the classroom. We wanted to find out how different groups of learners – male and female, pupils from different social classes, different ethnic groups and at different achievement levels – experienced their learning. We wanted to know what pupils could tell us about what it was like being a pupil trying to learn in the social dynamics of classroom life – about the social and educational dilemmas which characterise classrooms but which are rarely articulated in the hearing of their teachers.

We chose as our settings two rather different secondary schools. The inner city comprehensive (Mandela) drew on a diverse catchment of children from different minority ethnic backgrounds in a predominantly working-class community. The school had a history of mixed ability teaching but that had started to change after the introduction of the National Curriculum and SATs testing. The second school (Greenfield) was a large community college in a regional city with a catchment of predominantly white children from different socio-economic backgrounds. Pupils were placed in sets from Year 8 for the core National Curriculum subjects. In both schools we chose to focus on Year 8 pupils in one tutorial group, each with about 26 pupils.

Since the aim of the study was to discover how different groups of pupils experienced their learning in the classroom, we decided to use group discussions as the method of consultation. In both schools we were given considerable help by the form tutor to identify the groups, each of which included five or six pupils. Every child in the tutorial group was included in two group discussions. There were separate male and female groups of pupils who were clustered according to teachers' assessment of being higher, middle and lower achievers. Some of these groups were socially homogeneous, others had a mix of pupils from different socio-economic backgrounds. One of the middle-achieving groups in Greenfield was composed of female Asian working class pupils. In Mandela, all the groups, apart from the higher-achieving girls' group and the lower-achieving boys' group, were ethnically mixed.

In this account, we focus on the views of lower-achieving male pupils, all of whom, in these two schools, were white working class, and lower-achieving African-Caribbean and white working class girls.

Group consultation strategies with a diverse range of pupils are unlikely to elicit consensus and more likely to disclose different opinions and perspectives. The value of the exercise was precisely to hear those views on learning that may well not be tapped by everyday encounters with teachers. Group consultations can also probe whether particular teaching strategies are experienced as equally effective by all pupils. In this way, both consensus and difference in relation to teaching can be explored.

Whilst discussions about learning with groups of pupils are quite common in schools, the focus of our research was rather different. Unlike the project described earlier, this project took a sideways approach, using a sociological frame of reference rather than the professional frames of reference used by teachers. We drew upon and adapted the distinctions offered by Bernstein (1996) when he argued that it was very important to know to what extent pupils were able to participate fully and effectively in their own learning. He was concerned about the social inequalities in classroom life – about whose voice is actually heard in the 'acoustic of the school' and whether all learners have the same opportunities and rights. He asked whether all pupils:

- were called upon to voice their concerns
- were listened to by teachers
- had been given the confidence to learn
- felt that they belonged as individuals to the school community
- had the opportunity to control the procedures and practices that shaped their learning.

Bernstein clustered these ideas into what he called the three 'democratic pedagogic rights': **enhancement, inclusion** and **participation**. For our project, we drew up three sets of questions with which to consult pupils about these 'rights'.

Renaming the themes slightly, we framed questions to pupils around:

- feeling confident
- feeling included
- feeling in control.

This part of the project was theory led. Pupils were asked to respond to our set of questions but at certain points they generated new themes for us. They did not use us as a channel of communication to the teacher and it is unclear whether what they told us could have been generated by teachers consulting pupils directly. Pupils were not talking so much about actual teaching episodes but about their own experiences of teaching and learning in the classroom. By consulting pupils about the **social conditions of their learning** – the relationships between pupils and their teachers and between pupils themselves – we begin to hear what it is like to be a learner in the social world of the classroom. What they tell us in their own way is what is at stake for them as learners and just how complex learning relationships are (Cook-Sather, 2002). What they throw light on particularly is the relationship between the social conditions of learning and learning itself.

Of great importance for any teacher is the knowledge that what is being taught is understood and used effectively by pupils. Great reliance is therefore placed on successful communication strategies. We have selected from our wealth of data some pivotal examples of how lower-achieving pupils talked about their experiences of learning. These pupils were less successful in learning and, in communicating their learning problems, they might benefit most from pupil consultation strategies.

We also describe some of the data collected in the later stages of the project where individual pupils were asked to evaluate their learning in particular Maths and English lessons. The debriefing interviews focused on the processes of consultation and suggest that there is considerable mileage in developing effective consultation tools in order to enhance pupil learning.

Feeling confident

One of the first things we did was to consult the various groups of pupils about what they considered to be the distinction between the 'good' and 'bad' learner, how they described themselves and how they knew what sort of learner they were. We moved from there to discussing what might help them be successful in the classroom and whether they thought they could be more successful at school. Indirectly, their comments served as advice on what the teacher might do to help them become more successful in their learning.

Defining the good learner: 'ability' versus effort

A crude but nevertheless effective question is 'What makes a "good" or "bad" learner?'. Our discussions with pupils demonstrated how well they had incorporated the messages of the school about the characteristics of a good learner. In both schools, most pupils we consulted associated successful learners with features such as listening, hard work, being good at responding, concentrating, giving work in, making an effort, being liked by the teacher, and doing well. The higher-achieving children, however, were more likely to associate the term with enjoyment and 'being challenged', being liked by the teacher, knowing most subjects and being interested in schoolwork. This particular group of pupils talked about the act of learning rather than just gaining knowledge.

Lower-achieving boys at Greenfield were much more circumspect about the distinction between good and bad learners. The lower-achieving boys associated good learners with classroom learning behaviour – paying attention, not talking and doing the homework. Within these definitions they were able to rank themselves in terms of the amount they worked and the amount they talked in class. Most therefore ranked themselves around 5 on a scale of 1 to 10. So long as they made an effort, paid attention and did the work (even whilst talking a lot during class), they could be classified as good learners. In contrast, 'bad learners' were described as those who were on the wrong side of the behavioural tracks.

> **Carl:** *Dane and Jake are on zero because they're always mucking about and get barely any work completed.*
>
> **Craig:** *A bad learner mucks around and throws things across the classroom and doesn't listen at all.*

The language of learning which emerged from our consultations at Mandela was different. Here, most pupils appeared ambivalent about this distinction and only the three middle class boys were prepared to position themselves as good learners. In comparison with Greenfield pupils, who could draw information about themselves as learners from their position in various sets, the Mandela pupils were used to mixed-ability classrooms. They were less likely to use learner distinctions and more likely to place more emphasis on social variables such as gender or ethnic group. They were more ambivalent about describing themselves as good learners. The ways in which these pupils constructed differences between learners had implications for their confidence as learners. If learning is about effort then there is much that can be gained by hard work. The lower-achieving group of boys in Mandela underlined this point: It's important to focus, 'Yeah you need to focus a lot', and persist, 'You need to read over and over to get it done'.

Intelligence

Boys used the concept of intelligence to underscore the differences between learners. Working class boys, in particular, articulated a painful awareness of the readiness of schools to attribute successful learning to 'ability': they catalogued a range of innate factors which combine to exclude themselves. For example: 'You've got to be clever'; 'you have to be intelligent to be a good learner'; 'you have to be clever to get jobs, important jobs' – although for Ricky, there seems to be an element of individual volition: 'You've got to be in a good mood to be clever'. The danger for these boys was the role which such intrinsic qualities play in shaping their confidence. These lower-achieving working class boys were the only ones to describe invidious evaluations of their own intelligence:

> **Ricky:** Other people saying you are thick.
>
> **Robbie:** Yeah, telling you you're stupid.
>
> **Dean:** People undermine your confidence by putting you down.
>
> **Danny:** People putting you down makes you feel like you are thick and then you feel like you just don't want to try. Your feelings are hurt.

This undermining of their confidence, which all four boys articulated, was further exacerbated by 'being picked on' by teachers because, as Ricky pointed out: 'It makes you think – what's the point of trying?' These boys vividly described how they were made to feel stupid and childlike in classroom encounters with teachers:

> **Kenny:** *Some teachers are a bit snobby, sort of. And some teachers act as if the child is stupid. Because they've got a posh accent. Like they talk without 'innits' and 'mans', like they talk proper English. And they say, 'That isn't the way you talk' - like putting you down. Like I think telling you a different way is sort of good, but I think the way they do it isn't good because they correct you and make you look stupid.*

> **Martin:** *Those teachers look down on you.*

> **Kenny:** *Yeah, like they think you're dumb ... We don't expect them to treat us like their own children. We're not. But we are still kids. I'd say to them, 'You've got kids. You treat them with love but you don't need to love us. All you need to do is treat us like humans'.*

Setting

The organisation of teaching into a hierarchy of sets at Greenfield can have a similar effect of making some pupils 'feel stupid'. The working class boys in the lowest English sets also wondered whether there was any point in trying hard at their learning:

> **Neil:** *It's too easy, it's like they think you're stupid or something ...*

> **Sean:** *Yeah, like 'How do you write "the"?'*

> **Neil:** *I've got some cards like A, B, C, D with numbers on the top and it says stuff like what number is on B, and you just see it says 2 on it.*

> **Qu:** How does it make you feel when work is too easy?

> **Neil:** *Well it feels all right if you've done well and they're hard but things like that make you feel stupid and it's not that much of a challenge.*

> **Qu:** And you think it's a shame you can't work as hard as last year?

> **Neil:** *Yes, because like if we had it easy and you finish you don't feel real good because it's easy but if you have a hard one, you feel good with yourself because you have done it.*

Rather than using their own assessment of their learning (something which higher-achieving groups were confident to do), the lower-achieving groups sought reassurance for the quality of their work from their teachers, other pupils and their parents. Working class boys indicated their reliance on others to motivate them and assess whether they were doing well at school. They reported feeling most successful at learning when the teacher or their parents said 'Well done'.

Homework

Homework was represented as an important and sometimes critical element in sustaining confidence. Dean and Robbie, both lower-achieving pupils, comment:

> **Dean:** *Do homework to be a good learner.*

> **Robbie:** *Yeah, homework can help you.*

But there are situations when the homework appears to be the source of the problem rather than the solution:

> **Danny:** *Sometimes like not being able to do the homework. Because it's a bit, some of it's a bit, some bits are quite difficult and you can't do them.*

Working class boys also revealed the difficult moments when their parents' help has not been possible (eg on school Maths) or when it has, their assistance has been ridiculed. Carl claimed that when they asked their Dads about schoolwork and they got it wrong, his teachers say, 'Well, then, they must have been stupid or something like that'. Their trust in school is breached by such moments. Sean, also from a working class family, reveals the shame he felt in relation to his History homework when he did not understand what was required.

The teacher asked the pupils to write about Henry VIII:

> ... he gives you this like little sheet and it has got 'What can you say about this bloke?' And I say, 'He's got a beard'. 'Sorry Sean, detention. You have just put "He has got a beard"'.

Sean's homework reflected his Dad's response to a 'pointless' task:

> Like the other day it was, 'What can you tell me about this?' and I asked my Dad about it and he goes, 'Well what's the point of setting this? It's just a picture. What can you tell from it? That he wears clothes and he has got a hat?'

Schools have long been aware of the sometimes quite substantial differences in the culture, ethos and message of the home and the school (Lynch and Lodge, 2002). There has been much discussion about the differences in particular between working class homes and schooling and the synchrony of middle class families with the educational languages, approaches and expectations encouraged by teachers (Bernstein, 1977a; b). Yet it is rare that teachers have the opportunity to discuss such conflicts with pupils. Consulting working class pupils about their learning can bring these issues to the fore. For example, as Sean told us, 'My mum tells me something and teacher tells me different'. Craig is even more informative about the differences:

> Like your parents give you like different methods of learning and then when you come in school, they say something different and you get confused and then you mix it like together and then you get it like wrong because you get confused.

Looking for support

Friends can soften the discomfort and insecurity that pupils, as low achievers and as boys, experience in the classroom. When we asked pupils what would make them feel or be more successful in the classroom, lower-achieving working class boys suggested some teaching strategies but frequently they described the role of friends in helping them cope with what, for some boys, was not a developed or comfortable relationship with the teacher.

By consulting these boys it is possible to get a sense of just how often they see relationships with teachers as tense and fraught with difficulty and the supportive role which their peer group and friends play in mediating this relationship and encouraging their learning (Reay, 2002).

The working class boys at both Mandela and Greenfield believed that teachers did not trust them, especially in comparison with girls whom they favoured. Although some girls talked in class, they usually 'want to get on with their work'. As a result, teachers trusted them more and allowed them to sit together. As a consequence of having such trust, girls were seen as getting away with all sorts of breaches in the codes of conduct. As Neil explained:

> In my English class, it will be like a table full of girls that are always talking, then there will be me on my table. We talk quite a lot but they will move people from my table but when the girls are talking they won't move them.

If boys like Dane are late (because he has to get his brothers ready for school in the morning) then they could be in quite a lot of trouble: 'If you're late they think you've been walking and mucking around'. But one girl in class was always late and always left her bag on the table: 'If a boy did that he gets in trouble straight away'.

Moreover, when boys do make an effort, teachers can be critical and/or punitive and they are reluctant then to maintain their effort:

> Nick: It's like when they give you detention and think that you aren't trying hard enough and you're trying your hardest.
>
> Qu: ... that makes you want to try hard or not try any more?
>
> Nick: Not try any more because if you're trying your hardest you just give up.
>
> Neil: And some people have disabilities or something. They're not good at writing or something but they're doing their best and teachers give them detention because it's not neat or something.

If such social tensions in the relationships between teachers and pupils in the classroom exist, it is not surprising that pupils have difficulty in suggesting teacher strategies that might help their learning.

However, they clearly valued teachers who were quietly sensitive to their difficulties:

> **Nick:** *Like in Maths, my teacher, she writes a Maths sum up on the board and puts the answer in and as she goes along she explains it so that you understand how to put numbers in.*

> **Neil:** *One of my Maths teachers ... like he will help you because, like, some would put their hand up and he'll go to people who don't put their hand up and help them with it.*

Teachers tend to see talking to friends as evidence of lack of concentration and not as a source of support for learning (see Galton et al, 2003). Yet friends are very important to lower-achieving pupils in both schools. In pupils' minds, teachers do not realise that it is possible to work and talk and still be a reasonable sort of learner. Neil reported that he would be working 'but then I talk at the same time'; Craig commented: 'I talk but I usually get all my work done. Mark tries really hard but talks also'. Carl summarised the feelings of others in his group with this comment:

> *Talking helps me 'cos it makes me feel comfortable ... And when the teacher is kind of walking around you, you think they're kinda thinking you've done it wrong or something.*

Friends play many roles. They can cover up the effects of poor performance – by mediating the evaluation of your learning: they can tell you when you have done well and give you a reference point and they protect you from individual humiliation:

> *If you go in a group and if you're doing work in class ... you kinda feel more comfortable because if they get it wrong then you get it wrong and you aren't the only one.*

This reliance on friends is not just about friendship or social chat. Especially in the more fluid environment of the mixed-ability classes at Mandela, friends become the source of pupils' academic and social status. At the same time, social interaction can have a detrimental effect on a pupil's learning: 'If you don't like being in your class and all that, you become a bad learner' (Danny); 'Some people get on my nerves and then I get a bit sulky and my work goes down' (Dean). The social interactions of the classroom in this context become a critical element in classroom learning.

Summary

From these small slices of our data, it is possible to learn what it was like to be a working class lower-achieving boy in classrooms at Mandela and Greenfield. One striking aspect of the discussions was the vulnerability of working class boys in particular who appeared to have little to feel really confident about. During the discussions, they described their slowness in writing and their lack of understanding of the work set. Their interpretation of learning as behaviour, and of success as based on fixed intelligence, contributes to their insecurities in the classroom. They appear to feel misunderstood by teachers and on occasion unfairly treated, especially in contrast with girls; at the same time, they are heavily reliant (in contrast with the independent higher-achieving pupils we talked to) upon teachers' assessments of the quality of both their work and their ability. They appear far removed from the present ideal of the 'independent learner'. But it is important to recognise that, despite such difficult conditions for learning, even the least successful learners expressed a rather cautious yet, on the whole, a positive approach to learning – they wanted to learn and they wanted to do well.

Feeling included

Consulting pupils about classroom life has much to contribute to learning if it can throw light upon the interconnections between social identities and teaching. Each child's learning identity is constructed in relation to his or her other social identities. In some school contexts, these connections might not be very strong, especially if the school emphasises individual performance and motivation (and as we have already found, friendship provides a valuable source of support in competitive learning environments). However, in other school contexts, where classrooms are socially and culturally heterogenous, social groupings may play a much stronger role. We asked pupils whether they felt that teachers treated all alike or whether some groups were more likely to feel excluded in the classroom.

Gaining the teacher's attention

At Mandela, our consultations with pupils uncovered the complex ways in which different groups of pupils in the same classroom understood notions of fairness, particularly in terms of gaining teachers' attention. Working class pupils have to confront cultural dissonance between home and school of the sort described earlier and they have therefore a far harder task in order to fit comfortably within the official agenda of the school (Reay, 2002). This 'difficult fit' emerged strongly in what the working class children had to say about social inclusion in the classroom. Their narratives of pupil–teacher interaction configured a distanced, and hierarchical, relationship with their teachers. Although the middle-achieving, working class boys in Mandela were the more vocal and vociferous in their opposition to official schooling, the working class girls' sense of alienation was just as raw and tangible. A potent sense of unfairness infused their attitudes:

> **Jodie:** *Yeah, our English teacher. He likes the three clever girls a lot because they are always answering questions. He never gives other people a chance to say ...*

> **Carlene:** *If we put our hands up and we want to answer the question, the cleverest person, he will ask them, and we all know it's the right answer. And then he starts shouting at us saying that we are not answering.*

> **Jodie:** *Yeah, at parents' evening in Year 7, my dad came over and spoke to my English teacher. And he said that I don't put my hand up often to answer questions and take part in the lesson. And I was like OK, I'll start putting my hand up. And now I'm putting my hand up and he doesn't choose me, and I'm like what's going on here? And there's no point me taking part if he's not going to hear me out.*

This sense of unfairness in relation to teacher attention was found amongst most Mandela pupils who thought that groups other than themselves received disproportionate time and attention from the teacher. Besides 'the cleverest', those pupils who received most attention were thought to be the low-achieving children, and specifically the boys who received extra support from the Learning Support Centre. It was only two higher-achieving boys who felt that the distribution of teacher attention and time was fair. For most pupils, the failure to get enough positive attention was a critical aspect of their ability to learn in the classroom.

Middle- to lower-achieving working class girls perceived almost all the other social groups in the classroom as receiving preferential treatment from the teacher:

> **Candice:** *I think boys like Timi and Hasmi are seen as more important 'cos they're the goody-goodies.*
>
> **Carlene:** *And Paul and Dean because they get extra help.*
>
> **Alexa:** *And it's the clever girls as well, they get treated better than us.*
>
> **Candice:** *There are things I don't like about teachers and the main one is they have favourites and they let the clever girls do whatever they want.*
>
> **Jodie:** *Yes, Katherine, Megan and Laura.*
>
> **Carlene:** *And our English teacher loves Katherine. She can't do anything wrong.*

In addition these girls cited a further social grouping that sees itself as 'more important'. This male group of 'naughty people' prevented girls from learning by capturing the teacher's attention:

> **Carlene:** *It's unfair because the naughty boys stop us from learning because the teacher can't teach us.*
>
> **Lisa:** *And then the teacher will put 'Class very noisy' on the class sheet and it's not the whole class.*
>
> **Carlene:** *And then they'll say, 'I can't come and help you. I have to stand here and watch who is being naughty'. So they can't come round and help us. So the boys stop us learning better.*

However, from the perspective of the SEN boys and the 'popular' male pupils, it was not so much teacher attention that they received as high levels of regulation. Having teacher attention can be a two-edged sword! Kenny and Jason comment:

> **Kenny:** *The teacher doesn't ever give me any attention except for when I chat.*
>
> **Jason:** *Teachers notice me too much, but you don't want them to notice you for bad work, only good work.*

However, it can be a good thing to be noticed by teachers, especially if such attention helps them with learning and is not about behaviour:

> **Neil:** *It's quite important if the teacher does notice because say like you are stuck on a question, like – say you are stuck on something and you are too embarrassed to put your hand up and the teacher is like ...*
>
> **Carl:** *So if the teacher is looking at you they can see that you are struggling so they come and help you, instead of you putting your hand up and getting embarrassed.*

Craig captured the subtle differences in teacher attention:

> *Well sometimes it's a bad thing if the teacher keeps noticing you and you talk ... But it is good if you ... are like struggling and they notice you and then come and help you. If we say something she will try and understand it, like if we say it in slang or something.*

Wherever these boys sit, they were aware of teacher surveillance:

> **Sean:** *But there is front or back but if you are sitting in the front then the teacher is going to be staring at you all the time. If you sit at the back he'll be coming back over there ...*
>
> **Neil:** *He comes to the back when he is explaining something on the board and he'll say 'Oh what do you think about this ...' because he automatically thinks you are not listening to him if you are at the back.*

In the boys' accounts, the teaching of knowledge was often completely masked by issues of control:

> **Martin:** *Today, in Maths, yeah, this was a piece of paper like that, and it's got questions on it, and my friend was just going like that up against his face, and then the teacher said 'Don't wipe your snot; here's a thing to wipe your snot'. And he wasn't even doing that, he was just leaning on it, like that, while the teacher was talking. And he told him to get out and then he went outside and he didn't even close the door. And if that was me I would have just talked to the boy quietly and told him he was wrong to do that.*

> **Kenny:** *Yeah, he just shouted at him.*
>
> **Martin:** *He just shouted and made sure everyone could hear him ... 'cos he was in the wrong. But you can only get a teacher in the wrong if you've got proof. They can always get you because the other teachers don't believe kids.*

And again:

> **Matthew:** *The new [subject] teacher, she doesn't respect the way we learn 'cos some of us learn at a slower pace than others and she has no respect for the slower ones.*
>
> **Kenny:** *And she just treated us like a pile of shit, man.*

In contrast, these boys perceived the girls as the ones in the class receiving quality time from the teachers – what Martin called 'nice attention':

> **Martin:** *Girls get away with more than boys.*
>
> **Jake:** *They do.*
>
> **Leroy:** *Yeah, because the teachers don't expect them to muck about.*
>
> **Martin:** *They get nice attention.*

For the 'popular' boys and other middle-achieving boys in the class, the unfairness of teachers, and particularly the preferential treatment given to the girls, was a constant theme – resonating with Younger et al's (1999) findings:

> **Kenny:** *Some teachers are always sexist. They favour the girls because they think the boys are immature.*

And:

> **Martin:** *The teachers are nicer to the girls.*
>
> **Leroy:** *Sometimes they are put on praise because they are answering the questions.*
>
> **Kenny:** *Yeah, teachers should be fair. If they're not it's unfair to us. And if I think I'm being treated unfairly then I won't be fair to the teacher.*

Martin: *Yeah, it's mostly us that gets into trouble.*

And:

Jake: *Girls can be just as silly as the boys.*

Martin: *Yeah, but then they don't get into trouble.*

Kenny: *Yeah, it's mostly us that gets in trouble.*

Fractious peer group cultures

Most teachers are aware of the negative effects of strong peer cultures in the classroom but may not see how these small but significant interactions are constructed and how they present a continuous and engrossing interplay of resentment and challenge:

Qu: *Do you think people in your class get on with one another?*

Andy: *No, wars all the time.*

George: *It's true you get different little groups.*

Jake: *Lots of them and they have different wars in the classroom. It's like fights all the time.*

Qu: *So these groups don't get on with each other?*

George: *No way.*

Andy: *No, they don't.*

Such fractiousness expresses itself in terms of the differences among pupils in relation to learning requirements, competing needs and yardsticks by which to compare favourable or not favourable attention by teachers. Moreover, the social hierarchies of the classroom exacerbate the divisions. Here, some middle class, higher-achieving pupils comment on the social dynamics of the classroom:

Katherine: *Some people are definitely seen as more important in our class.*

> **Megan:** *But it depends on what they are seen as more important for. Some people seem more important because they have to be helped a lot with their learning. So they get helped a lot more and shown what to do better.*
>
> **Laura:** *But also just in terms of class relationships people think they're more important if they are more popular.*
>
> **Jasmine:** *Not the girls so much. It affects the boys more.*
>
> **Laura:** *Yeah, definitely.*

The dominance of these localised peer group cultures in the school can of course shift the pupils' attention away from the teaching. Even our small-scale consultations revealed that in Mandela, being clever in 'official' ways was denigrated and, as Laura asserted, 'to be popular as a boy you have to be clever in different ways' – ways that validated the 'local' rather than the 'official' line on learning (see also Willis, 1977). The mismatch between the power of local peer group cultures and the official agenda of the school diverted attention away from learning.

The sense that cleverness marginalises you within the male peer group is reinforced by the identification, in all the focus groups, of the two most studious (and most middle class) boys as the two pupils who were most regularly marginalised or rejected. Lisa summed up the collective feeling of the rest of the class when she asserted 'No one likes the geeks'. The class tutor agreed: 'There's two or three middle class boys who have sacrificed any kind of social standing in order just to get on with their work'. When consulted, these boys asserted that they received adequate attention and a reasonable amount of praise. Unlike all the other pupils they were content with the seating arrangements (see next section), and felt they were treated fairly by the teachers. In contrast to the rest of their peer group, they had a strong sense that they were heard within the classroom context. Their comments showed that they were well aware of the social dynamics and that they acted strategically to preserve a sort of equilibrium for themselves:

> **Hasmi:** *Being noticed can be good or bad. It all depends on what you're doing. Like even if you don't know what to do you might not want to be noticed. If you know what you have to do and you want to put your hand up for a question then it's good to be noticed. Just in case it's right or wrong. So you know in the future. Like you can check out whether you*

understand properly. And you'll remember stuff if you put your hand up. Like if you just hear other people say it you don't remember it as well, but if you said it yourself you will remember more. That's what I find anyway.

Where you sit matters!

Organising a classroom that is suited to learning for all pupils is one of the many challenges teachers face on a day-to-day basis. For some, this involves intervening to manage social tensions between groups of pupils and also individual personalities. Teachers might determine the seating arrangements, like seating boys next to girls, or they might allow friends to sit together. What is clear is that pupils pick up all sorts of messages from classroom seating policy – about being trusted by the teacher, for instance – and this can increase their anxieties about learning, particularly if the prescribed seating appears to lead to their being under teacher scrutiny.

In Greenfield, the seating policies varied from teacher to teacher and showed that teacher-imposed seating or free choice were safeguards against disruption:

> **Neil:** Like in some lessons the teacher puts you in alphabetical order or like boy, girl and there wouldn't be much messing around but like in some lessons teachers don't really mind because it is good to be next to your friends and there is quite a lot of mucking around and talking.
>
> **Qu:** So you think there is less mucking around if the teacher chooses seats for you?
>
> **Neil:** Yes.

The others in the discussion group, however, suggested that learning worked less well when these boys were separated from their friends:

> **Tony:** I get bored if I'm not with my friends.
>
> **Carl:** You would see quite a lot of rubbers going across the room. Every time the teacher turns her back on a naughty one then that person will throw something. It always happens.
>
> **Neil:** People climbing out of their seats.

The responses demonstrate that pupils think a lot – and quite strategically – about the meanings of seating patterns and they find teachers predictable in their responses to pupils who sit 'at the back' or 'at the front':

> **Carl:** *The teacher will get suspicious if you are up to something at the back and they can't see you that well, but if you are at the front, you won't muck about so much because you are right in front of them and they think you wouldn't dare talk 'cos you are right in front of them.*
>
> **Qu:** *Do people at the front get extra learning?*
>
> **Carl:** *No 'cos say you are in the back, you are working and the teacher keeps on looking at you and you get a bit nervous.*
>
> **Neil:** *And distracted.*
>
> **Qu:** *Distracted? You are aware of the teacher watching you?*
>
> **Neil:** *Mmm.*
>
> **Qu:** *So distraction, Craig, would you agree?*
>
> **Craig:** *I hate it when they like breathe on you!*
>
> **Qu:** *Is there a place in the classroom that's best for learning?*
>
> **Craig:** *Middle.*
>
> **Sean:** *Middle.*
>
> **Neil:** *Gotta be the middle.*
>
> **Dane:** *Yeah.*

They elaborated on the 'map' of seating/surveillance possibilities:

> **Sean:** *[In the middle] you can get on with your work and you can hear him.*
>
> **Carl:** *... And they don't get, they don't kind of snoop.*
>
> **Sean:** *But if you are next to a window you can't really work because you keep looking out of the window.*

In the following comments, these boys described the threat of girls surrounding them, isolating them from their male support in a context in which they were already discomfited by the threat of being asked questions, by being watched at every point by the teacher – and by learning itself. If, in the corridor, the boys are held back by the teacher the girls get into the classroom first and they seize the middle ground – or worse, one boy gets in and the girls swarm in and surround him!

> **Sean:** *Girls get there first ... They let the girls in first ... 'You stand over there', if you have been talking in the line.*

> **Carl:** *... They let the girls go and sit in all the good spaces in the middle so we have to sit in the front or the back.*

> **Neil:** *And we choose the back.*

> **Craig:** *It's better than the front.*

Treating everyone the same

The pupils in Greenfield engaged in discussion about whether all pupils should be treated the same. Nick, Neal and Sean, for example, pointed out that in reality pupils were not treated the same and the girl–boy dimension was particularly strong; girls sometimes got more opportunities – in this case opportunities not to be punished.

> **Neil:** *You hardly hear about a girl getting detention.*

> **Sean:** *No, if you go in detention there're all boys.*

Girls, according to boys, seemed to get 'more chances'; even though the official rhetoric of the school was that they treated all pupils alike:

> **Neil:** *Differently. Well some of the teachers they all treat like the girls and boys the same but if there are boys talking they will be more likely to get split up but if it's a group of girls, they will have five warnings before they get split up.*

> **Craig:** *And when they do, they only split up a couple of people, not the whole lot.*

Their views confirm many other studies about the frequency of punishment and discipline for boys in schools (Arnot et al, 1998; Gillborn and Mirza, 2000; Wright, 2000).

> **Qu:** *What do teachers do generally?*
>
> **Neil:** *Give us detention or warning like, say, 'If you do that again you'll be in after school'.*
>
> **Nick:** *In English if you forget your book you get strikes. If you forget your book once you get the first strike, second strike is a ten-minute detention and third strike you get 30 minutes.*
>
> **Qu:** *And is that every term or half-term? How many times?*
>
> **Sean:** *The whole year.*

Our discussions with these pupils revealed the endless round of social and educational dilemmas which characterise classrooms but which are rarely articulated in the hearing of their teachers. Where detentions follow poor classroom behaviour, pupils are then disconnected from their friends. Friends as we have seen are their survival strategy. Boys understand therefore that the consequences of poor behaviour are the cause of their own social – and educational – exclusion:

> **Carl:** *If you misbehave ... if they talk or something then they get split up from their friends 'cos if you talk a little, well if you have got kind of a reputation of being bad, if you talk a little bit, they split you up. You can't work without your friends basically ...*

When we asked what teachers do that leaves some pupils feeling left out of learning, they responded:

> **Craig:** *[They] split you up.*
>
> **Carl:** *[They] keep looking at you.*
>
> **Neil:** *You say like your own answer and they keep going to someone else, they don't go to you.*

What would be the alternative? Neil, Carl and Sean had some suggestions about how the teacher can make sure all are included:

Neil: *Say, 'Well done. You are doing really good'.*

Carl: *Give merits.*

Sean: *Or using, like ... saying, 'You should be doing this right now – just like Adam or something like that'. And then you think 'I am doing that right'.*

Feeling in control

Pupil dependency on the teacher for evaluation of learning and for initiating positive learning experiences contrasts with much of the emphasis today upon the notion of the 'independent learner'. Pupils are now expected to take responsibility for their own learning and, by implication, be able to control their progress by increasing their motivation and effort and thus learning 'when required'. But do pupils have any sense of control over their own learning? By consulting pupils about how far this is the case, teachers may be able to uncover more of the complex relationship between their teaching and pupils' learning. This relationship is most clearly seen in terms of how far pupils believe that they can have a say in the content of what they are taught or have choices within subjects or about activities. Teachers might wish to explore, as we did, the extent to which different groups of pupils feel able to control the pace of their learning by asking teachers to adapt the pace of their teaching.

Below we demonstrate the value of consulting pupils on these themes. We focus again on the experiences of the least successful pupils in order to illustrate how consultation might enable us to rethink the organisation of their classroom experiences. Pupils link their view that not all the knowledge they are being taught in schools is relevant or valuable to whether they consider it worth the effort.

Judging the relevance of the curriculum

Some pupils recognise the degree of governmental control over teachers in relation to the curriculum and may believe that their difficult relationships with teachers stem from the fact that teachers are under serious pressure to succeed in performance terms. For these pupils it appears pointless for them to assume that they will have any real control over the nature of their expected learning.

Some working class boys at Mandela were so ambivalent about the content of the curriculum that 'choice' was irrelevant:

> Qu: *If you had a choice what would you choose to learn?*
>
> Jason: *Nothing.*
>
> George: *Nothing.*
>
> Andy: *No idea.*
>
> Paul: *Definitely nothing.*

The only time these boys did articulate a positive relationship to knowledge was when they talked about those aspects of learning which engage the body as well as the mind:

> Andy: *Drama's still fun but most of the other work is boring.*
>
> George: *Yeah, Drama's good.*
>
> Andy: *It's mostly acting and there's more focus on doing something rather than writing something down and copying from a book.*
>
> George: *Yeah, you get to move around and do stuff, so that's more fun.*

They distinguish between enjoyable activities which satisfy their preference for short, discrete tasks that include an element of competition, and book-based learning which is unanimously described as 'boring'. These pupils are talking about learning in the social context of the group discussion and it is difficult to disentangle their genuine feeling of estrangement from much of the knowledge on offer from the pressures of the peer group to appear 'cool' in front of each other (see also Frosh et al, 2002). Jason's claim that most of the boys spend their time 'ninety nine point nine mucking around, point one working', can be largely attributed to exaggeration and bravado, but it also indicates a wider male peer group in which school-based knowledge is given a low value. Certainly, school forms of knowledge appear to be a major problem for some pupils and only seem to have been resolved satisfactorily for these boys in the teaching and learning of French (somewhat against the national pattern – see Jones et al, 2001):

> **Leroy:** *Like French, yeah, she gave us games and the other day she gave us a book to do and the next day she gives us a worksheet about sort, search and stuff, and the next day we ...*
>
> **Martin:** *It'll be back to games.*
>
> **Leroy:** *... she writes stuff on the board and we have to pronounce it. And at the end, if we have time, she's always letting us play a game.*
>
> **Jake:** *That's more interesting.*
>
> **Kenny:** *It's teaching all different stuff.*
>
> **Leroy:** *In my subject list I put French on top ...*
>
> **Martin:** *Like, we played a game today and what it was, we had this sheet ...*
>
> **Kenny:** *The game is like a competition ...*
>
> **Jake:** *Yeah, it was fun.*

Competition was represented to us as important for the boys as long as it had little to do with serious study and was converted into non-threatening 'fun and games'. School-based learning is only acceptable in disguised forms: learning has to be served up as if it is not learning for these boys to take any pleasure in it (see Younger and Warrington, 1999). There are also resonances here with Hey et al's (2000) analysis of learning identities which can lead to a self-sabotaging scenario of 'Can't win, won't win and don't want
to play'.

The discussions also revealed oppositions to school knowledge which emphasised the value of popular cultural forms which appeared more relevant to life:

Kenny: *A lot of what you learn in school isn't relevant, like it doesn't help you with your life.*

Andy: *Like you learn loads of important stuff out of school like catchphrases and stuff off the television and how to improve your football skills.*

Jason: *And technology things and I'm learning Chinese.*

Paul: *I'm learning to do tricks on bikes. BMXing.*

Neil wanted more practical knowledge linked to employment whilst Craig wanted both relevance and 'fun', such as using *Blackadder* in history lessons. Similar themes were found amongst the high-achieving boys at Mandela. All found Art interesting 'all of the time'; 'Science is quite interesting because you get to do experiments' (Timi); 'Most of the time French, games and PE and Drama's good most of the time because you get to act' (Hasmi); 'Technology's good too' (Timi). But they also asserted that knowledge gleaned outside of school was just as important: 'Like Pokemon you learn hand–eye coordination and making your brain quicker, stuff like that, that's just as important.' Except for the high-achieving boys, what emerged from the boys' talk was an instrumentality and an ambivalence towards school-based knowledge and learning.

Controlling the pace of learning

When consulted, pupils are able to reveal how they struggle to control their own learning. If the pace is too slow, there is clearly the danger of boredom or disengagement – even anger because they could be insulted by such low expectations. If the pace is too fast, then it might be difficult to keep up, to understand in any depth, to catch the instructions for a class activity or for homework. Getting it right, however, in a classroom filled with different learners – and, in the case of mixed ability teaching, of different learning levels – is difficult. By consulting pupils, we can begin to learn how they experience the pace of learning and how much they feel they can adapt or modify the teacher's pace. The differences in what the pupils had to say was particularly strong on this topic.

Whilst it is common knowledge that (working class) boys in particular can disrupt lessons, attracting nearly all the teacher's time and energy, it has generally been thought that such disruption is a sign of disaffection (Skelton, 2001; Epstein et al, 1998). Our discussions with pupils around control of learning suggest that the story is more complicated. Those pupils are deeply dependent on the teacher in terms of their learning and confidence, and appear to have little if any control over the pace of learning. These are pupils who seek power through other strategies. They use as many opportunities as possible to keep the teacher's attention whilst clearly worrying about the disciplining elements and surveillance that they receive by way of return. Teachers in their eyes need to control events (and should do according to these boys); they do not appear to be all that happy with disruptions to their own learning that, ironically, they have often initiated.

Thus, the majority of the male working class pupils seemed to be learning that knowledge was something beyond, rather than within, their control. While a few gave the impression that they were able to have the teacher adjust the pace of lessons to fit their needs, not all boys were so successful. The low-attaining working class boys felt they had little control over the teacher:

> **Dean:** *Some teachers, they write it on the board and then they say it really fast. Teachers, like, they should explain it more clearly, more slowly.*
>
> **Paul:** *When you're just on the last line he rubs it off quick.*
>
> **Dean:** *Before you've managed to write it all down!*
>
> **Paul:** *Teacher should wait. Or write it down for you.*

Getting stuck, particularly in English and Mathematics, and being unable to get sufficient support brought learning to a halt. Central to these boys' assumptions was that their learning required additional teacher support.

By consulting pupils on control over learning, we discovered just how thin the line was between 'showing up' boys by giving them work that was too difficult or too easy and supporting them. Although easy work allowed these boys to be educationally productive, something they normally struggled to achieve, it also generated ambivalence:

Ricky: *You sometimes get too much easy work in Maths and it's below your level, and you ain't learning nothing.*

Robbie: *Because you already know it.*

Ricky: *And that's not good.*

Most of the time they seemed to find it really hard to admit when work was too hard. Rather, they claimed that they 'just can't be bothered'. They engaged in avoidance tactics, as the girls had noticed, to ensure the work was not too challenging – despite protestations that challenge was what they 'really' wanted. Yet, they also recognised that when they managed to get away with making less effort than they were capable of, they were in effect letting themselves down. These contradictions were vividly illustrated by a desire to control but, ironically, not necessarily in ways that supported their learning. The working class boys' reports suggested that their attempts to control pacing had negative consequences both in terms of their identity and their achievement. The anger of the lower-achieving working class boys at Mandela about what some considered irrelevant knowledge or pointless activities and a lack of control over their learning was clearly in evidence.

In Greenfield classrooms, opportunities to comment on the pace, in the context of setting by attainment, were also fraught with difficulty. Pupils could be laughed at, shouted at, but even more significantly pupils could be dropped a set if shown to be unable to 'keep up' (interestingly, no pupil in our study talked about the possibility of being raised a set). Their sphere of agency (the ability to choose their course of action) in controlling the pace of learning was therefore constrained, especially for those who were thought to have the most difficulty in learning. They were happy to keep the lesson too slow (this made it easy) but as Alice said, 'If they're going too fast then you're then thinking 'Oww! They're going to think I'm really dumb!'.

Girls in the lower sets tried to reshape the relationship with teachers by seeking an appropriate **style** of communication:

Carrie: *I might say 'Sir' or it may be 'Miss'. 'If you don't mind me saying, could you speed up a bit 'cos I feel like I'm a ...'*

Jemima: *Snail.*

Kelly: ... *I think if someone's going really slow [laughter] I'd feel like saying: 'God, Sir, I'm not a dunce'. 'Cos they sort of treat us like it – 'cos you're thinking 'God, I'm not dumb, Sir! We can take it going a bit faster'. It's like you feel dumb. You say 'Sir, please can you go a bit faster, please?' Being polite.*

Meanwhile, Carrie needed to find a way of slowing the teacher down fearing that otherwise she would miss out:

You can get a really good education otherwise 'cos, like, they say, 'Copy this into your books and then you can revise it for a test'. Then you're still writing it and they're rubbing it off and writing something else. And they before you've even wrote that they're rubbing it off again, so I think you should be able to tell them.

The group of lower-achieving boys in Greenfield similarly reported to us that they had little control over what they learnt, the choice of what they did in class and the speed of learning – and they saw little opportunity for communication or consultation with the teacher. As Craig admitted, sometimes the teacher will say, 'Tell me if I am going too fast or something', but for most of these boys the opportunity was not real. Like the working class girls, if boys tried to slow the teacher down, there was the danger that 'people laugh at you'. Moreover, the culture of resistance was so ingrained that it could not easily be broken. As Adam pointed out, when teachers asked you to do something, these boys did the 'opposite' – the others agreed:

Sean: *If they say, 'Don't muck around' you will muck around. So you muck around because you kind of don't agree with the teacher ever.*

Neil: *Yeah, I remember in PE earlier he goes, 'You can now talk, just so I can sort this out'. And it was silent. It was absolutely silent.*

If such a relationship of non-cooperation exists, there is likely to be little incentive to establish other consultation methods: if the boys **are** offered more opportunities to control the pace of their learning, would they feel obliged not to cooperate?

Asking teachers to slow down the pace of teaching in high ability sets is less fraught with danger for higher-achieving boys. Some pupils manage apparently to shout out 'Slow down' especially when they are copying and they haven't finished. On the other hand, if teachers are going too slow there may be a case for not challenging the pace. As Robert commented, 'Brilliant. I recommend they go slow because you've got more time to write down the questions and think about it'.

Asking for help

Consulting pupils about the nature and type of control they feel they have over learning reveals that asking for teachers' help is a problem for a number of different groups. If the work was too difficult or the pace too fast, Carlene and Candice turned away from asking for help (it would be interesting to speculate on whether the fact that they were black and working class influenced these girls' sense of distance from a predominantly white middle class staff):

> **Candice:** I'm not really comfortable asking for help from the teacher. I don't know why. But it's because they don't listen to you. I just prefer to talk to my mum and dad and my brother.

> **Carlene:** With your parents, because with your parents you've got a special bond. You can tell them stuff. With the teacher you don't have anything. You can't exactly tell them how you feel, that you're stuck on something; you can't actually speak to them.

For them, boys' attempts to control the classroom verged on the manipulative. They saw boys as employing strategies of disaffection, indifference or illness. As Carlene said, all boys have to do is 'just sit back in their chairs and the teachers will write it down for them – so they don't ever make any effort'. When boys asked for more 'grammar, verbs and stuff' it was what they had already covered. As Candice and Carlene pointed out, the class was meant to have moved on long ago:

> **Candice:** That's what you are meant to learn in the first year. I can understand them teaching us in the first year, Year 7, but going onto Year 8 we are still learning it ...

> **Carlene:** *Things that we've never learnt about before, then we'd be interested to learn about it, but things that we already know, it's boring.*

Working class lower-achieving boys at Greenfield also spoke about their difficulties in asking for the teacher's help, but for different reasons. For example, if the teacher did not listen they could not use the teacher's technique of saying, 'What did I just say?'. This and other inconsistencies in teachers' behaviour damaged their trust. Not only did teachers not listen, but they also expected to be listened to.

However, our consultation suggested that this element of suspicion between boys and teachers, and the failure to communicate, was not something that was found only amongst working class boys. Higher-achieving upper middle class boys at Greenfield also believed that their strategies for slowing down the lesson were not necessarily effective:

> **Robert:** *Some do, some don't listen – say if you go, 'I'm not very good at that' or maybe 'I need more work on that'. Sometimes they just don't listen, they just carry on with another topic or something …*

> **John:** *Our teacher she is really stubborn. You put your hand up and she looks at you and she just looks away. This made me really angry … if I'm stuck on a question and I can't do it and she doesn't come over and help me, I just have to ask my friend.*

In sum, the problem as described by pupils was that teachers are not consistent in their response to pupils. Teachers are in command but they seem to pupils to be sometimes arbitrary in the way they exercise their power.

Summary

Pupils were often aware that neither they nor their teachers had control over the **content** of lessons; curriculum content was mainly determined by national bodies. This could affect the motivation of working class pupils in particular who wanted a curriculum which had more 'useful' knowledge. In relation to the **pace** of classroom learning, it was the higher-achieving middle class pupils, especially girls, who were the most likely group to feel that they had some degree of discretion over the way they were taught or how they learned. It was clear that different groups of pupils had developed different strategies for slowing down or speeding up the pace of learning to suit their particular needs, although these did not always work. Thus, whilst the democratic discourse of helping **all** pupils to be independent and autonomous learners is persuasive, in practice, it is not class-neutral; lower-achieving working class pupils are the least likely to feel that they have control over their own learning and the usual methods of communicating with teachers are not always effective for these pupils.

Asking pupils about the control of teaching and learning shows, for example, that pupils:

- don't want to be rude to the teacher
- don't want to lose their place in an attainment set
- don't want to show the rest of the class that they can't do the work
- don't think the teacher will listen
- feel they can't get the teacher to focus on their needs because of others' disruption
- are nervous lest they make the teacher angry
- believe they can only make a temporary difference by speaking out.

Those who arguably most need to control learning appeared to experience the least control over their learning. The only methods of seizing control of their learning for lower-achieving working class boys appeared to be manipulation of the teachers' attention through disruptive behaviour – and this could have negative effects on their learning.

Teachers' and pupils' views of consultation

The second stage of our project involved teachers more directly in consultation by inviting pupils to evaluate their Maths and English lessons. Using a simple evaluation sheet (see the box on page 73) they rated on a scale of 1 to 5 the pace, levels of interest and difficulty of the lesson which they had just had. They were also asked to rate their own understanding and learning in the lesson. This approach was novel for teachers and pupils. The debriefing interviews showed how pupils valued being consulted by their teachers. Pupils also confirmed our sense of the importance of recognising both the diversity of experience in the classroom and the personal and social vulnerabilities involved when talking about their learning to teachers.

Please tell me how you found the lesson by circling one number for each line								
The pace of the lesson	Too slow	1	2	3	4	5	Too fast
The interest of the lesson	Very low	1	2	3	4	5	Very high
Difficulty of the lesson	Too easy	1	2	3	4	5	Too difficult
My understanding	Very low	1	2	3	4	5	Very high
My learning	Very poor	1	2	3	4	5	Very good
Name .... Lesson .... Date								

The advantages of consultation

In Mandela, all the focus groups apart from the highest achieving (often upper middle class pupils) expressed very positive feelings about being consulted. Three working class boys commented:

> **Andy:** *It was good like being asked how you felt about stuff.*
>
> **Danny:** *It sort of made you feel important.*
>
> **Kenny:** *I liked doing the sheets because we talked about our viewpoints which we mostly don't get to do. And it gave us a chance to speak for ourselves not just sit in a corner and listen to the teacher.*

In contrast, the highest achieving pupils (both boys and girls) in each school were rather nonchalant about consultation, possibly because they felt that, unlike less successful pupils, they had a voice and felt more in tune with the school's purposes. They were able to manage informal dialogue between themselves and their teachers. The most dependent learners required the greatest maturity in handling their relationships with teachers, especially if their work – and classroom behaviour – was not in line with teacher expectations. Of particular importance for these pupils therefore was the problem of achieving some sort of 'communicative competence' in the classroom setting. Next, we describe how pupils were very aware of the skills needed to traverse this rocky terrain.

Communicative competence

Many pupils reported difficulty in responding when asked about their learning – often replying in standard ways, such as 'It's all fine'. Pupils admitted to saying 'only good things' when asked by teachers. Strategically, such 'politeness' serves to keep the teacher 'sweet'. Carrie, for example, was hindered by her view that it was rude to criticise people:

> **Qu:** *Do you think now you would be able to tell the teacher what he could do to help improve your learning?*
>
> **Carrie:** *No 'cos it would be like 'Uh I don't think you're teaching me right, you should do that and that'. They might get offended.*
>
> **Qu:** *Would that be bad?*
>
> **Carrie:** *Yeah.*
>
> **Qu:** *Why?*
>
> **Carrie:** *Because it's not nice, if you say, like, 'Your lesson is rubbish' and they'll ... like get upset about it.*

Pupils are also aware that talking to teachers requires considerable interpersonal skills and sensitivities because of their power and their moods. Some pupils were afraid of repercussions were they to inform teachers that their lessons were not effective:

> **Qu:** *Do you think you can tell the teacher what you think about his lessons, if you did not like his lesson?*
>
> **Kylie:** *[laughs] I probably wouldn't ... if you did he may shout at you.*
>
> **Qu:** *Why?*
>
> **Kylie:** *I don't know, he'd be like, if you told him he'd probably be angry. But maybe on these sheets ... but like if you write 'Oh I didn't like this lesson – maybe you can do a bit better' (and give an example), he wouldn't be so angry.*
>
> **Qu:** *Do you think there's a difference between writing it and telling him?*

Kylie: *Yeah, yeah.*

Qu: *Why?*

Kylie: *He can't shout.*

Kelly believed that the teacher would say 'If you can't say anything nice, then get out of my class':

Qu: *You don't feel free to criticise?*

Kelly: *No, I don't. That's why I like these sheets.*

Qu: *So, writing it down.*

Kelly: *Yeah, it's a lot easier because it's kind of different.*

Qu: *You could tell him on these sheets?*

Kelly: *Yeah, its less scarier.*

Qu: *What did you think you learnt by filling these sheets out?*

Kelly: *I think I learnt, like, how to say what I feel, but in a nice way, without offending anybody, and to tell the truth.*

Nick, a working class pupil, remained wary even in the written evaluation and gave a middle '3' rating for all items in order to make the teacher 'feel good'. The danger of falling out with the teacher was, for him, serious. In such cases, evaluation sheets may need to be anonymous but handwriting can of course disclose identity. The problem with existing modes of questioning pupils in the classroom was, as Abby pointed out, that some pupils were more able to speak the language of school and were therefore listened to more by the teacher:

Abby: *... I think the teachers listen to, like who knows the most ... because the naughty people ... because they don't like care ... [then] there's people who actually want to learn; they know what to do but they just don't somehow and then there's bottom people are like 'Please help' ... then the teacher's actually busy with the top group because they find it easier to talk to them instead of the others.*

Qu: Why?

Abby: *I think it's because of detail, because they just say the same language to the top people and then to like lower people, the bottom set, when they talk they find it harder, hard or something like that. A bit long, they have to say the same thing over and over again.*

Formal, non-verbal consultation processes have a particular value for pupils who are not adept in using existing modes of classroom communication effectively. Below we suggest how much less successful pupils would value a chance to evaluate their learning in particular lessons and their own progress, using consultative mechanisms.

Taking responsibility for your learning

Attempts by teachers to use a friendly and casual approach are welcomed by pupils and many pupils respond well to teachers who take the time to chat with them and write positive comments on their work. At Greenfield, pupil learning and achievement was understood to be the responsibility of individuals – pupils had learnt the mantra of self-responsibility and those that were able to reflect on their abilities independent of their teachers valued the exercise of self-evaluation sheets. Giving themselves scores meant that some pupils were motivated to try and improve their learning:

Qu: *Are there ways that doing these sheets have improved your learning?*

Kelly: *Well, yeah, in a way, 'cos you think, 'Have I really learnt anything?' and then you think, 'Well, I'm not sure, maybe' or 'Yeah, I have'. And then next lesson you come and you think, 'Well, the last lesson I learnt a lot, I want to learn a lot this lesson'. And then so on, so on, so on. You want, like, to do you best, don't ya? You think 'I want to do better than this' so you put more effort.*

Nick, who often got into trouble and was in the lower sets, also valued the activity but was concerned to please the teacher, not so much through what he said on the forms but through his working harder:

Qu: *Did you mind filling in the sheet?*

Nick: *Not at all, it was helping me realise what I was thinking about my Maths.*

Qu: What do you think you learnt by filling these sheets out?

Nick: *I learned that I can make it, that I could try to do my best, even on a bad day, because that would make the teacher happy, my parents and me happy. Even if it's not my main subject, if there's no interest in it.*

Qu: Are there ways that doing these sheets have improved your learning?

Nick: *Yes, it's given me a lot of time, on those three sheets, to think about what I've been doing and how it affected my learning in other classes, and in Maths, and how it affected the teacher thinking about me.*

Similarly, Craig, struggling in English, found that filling in the evaluation sheets 'made me think' and connect his learning to what was happening in the class. He described the exercise as 'fun' and 'interesting' – 'It's better, I saw what I did'. He was able to say 'what I don't understand' and 'what I am learning'. The evaluation sheets helped Craig and John to see the progress they were making over several lessons, as John said, 'Writing it down and looking back on it, seeing that I've been doing pretty well. I know that I can do the work he sets me'. Other pupils suggested that more questions should be added to the form for suggestions on how to change the lesson.

This desire for reflection on learning helps to define the potential of consultation techniques. At the same time, there remains the problem of the lack of trust between teacher and pupils which in some settings can limit or threaten consultation practices. In Mandela, some pupils appreciated the learning evaluation tasks but honesty may give way to strategic action:

Leroy: *Sometimes I put, 'It was very good' so you stay in the teacher's good books. They are asking for your true opinion, but obviously you can't give them your true opinion, otherwise they will dislike you and always watch out for you.*

Kenny: *Yeah, yeah, you couldn't be truthful.*

Qu: So you never get a chance to voice your opinions in the school?

Leroy: *No.*

Kenny: *'Cos we're all seen as fools.*

Leroy: *Like people treat you like fools, but they still teach you.*

Kenny: *Teachers think – I'm the King, you are my slave. I teach you. I tell you what to do, I tell you what to get, you get it. So it's sort of like – I'm the teacher, you are the pupil, I tell you what to learn and you learn it. But it ain't that easy.*

If a pupil is disaffected, alternative models of consultation may be seen as 'just another piece of paper'. Natalie is the one exception in the Greenfield group who had serious doubts about the value of the consultation exercise. She struggles with English and this self-evaluation sheet was seen by her as yet another English task that was overly challenging:

Qu: *Do you mind filling in the sheet?*

Natalie: *Yeah.*

Qu: *You did mind?*

Natalie: *Yeah, I did mind. I didn't want to do it.*

Qu: *Why?*

Natalie: *'Cos I didn't know, like some of the wording it was too hard. Didn't want to do it.*

Qu: *What do you think you learnt by filling these sheets out?*

Natalie: *Don't know. Nothing really.*

Qu: *Do you think it changed how you were learning?*

Natalie: *No, just some paper and we had to fill this sheet out. I wasn't learning anything ... it's just a piece of paper really.*

Natalie's experience of having asked for help and not receiving it, with teachers focusing on her behaviour and not her academic needs, meant that there was no trust to back up the self-evaluation consultation strategy.

If teachers introduce consultation techniques which do not allow for reflection they are experienced as irrelevant – for instance, if they give out the sheets as the bell goes so that pupils have no time to think about their learning. Nick and Craig, both working class pupils, enjoyed the activity but wished they had more time:

> **Nick:** *I would have preferred having time to think about all the classes, how they should be, what we can actually do.*

> **Craig:** *We had to do it in a minute, because like when he gave it to us, we couldn't concentrate on it. You didn't really have time to do it.*

Insufficient time to complete the evaluation form merely confirmed most pupils' lack of control over their learning:

> **Danny:** *It was annoying though because like, every ... like, we was late for our next lesson 'cos he did it at the last minute.*

> **Dean:** *He didn't give you enough time to fill it out.*

> **Robbie:** *And he was rushing us.*

> **Ricky:** *You get the sheet and he was – 'You have to hurry up now. You have to hurry up'.*

> **Dean:** *Didn't give us enough time to fill them out.*

> **Danny:** *Didn't give us enough time to think about what you are doing.*

> **Dean:** *So you have to quickly rush it.*

> **Hasmi:** *He only gives you about 30 seconds.*

> **Ben:** *If you got five minutes you could really think about – Am I really good at learning or ...?*

> **Balo:** *Then it would be worth it if you had enough time.*

Teachers' views on consulting pupils about their learning

The teachers in Greenfield and Mandela acknowledged the values of formal pupil consultation but the evaluation task raised issues about whether teachers could sustain high levels of consultation.

Mr Watson (a newly qualified teacher) said that, although he now planned 'to ask the kids how they think they learn', until now, he 'hadn't ever thought of doing that'. He valued the idea of consultation and saw, as a new teacher, the potential it offered for improving his lessons and extending his teaching repertoire. However, he was aware of the difficulties of incorporating pupil voice into the positive and friendly relationship with pupils he prided himself on and therefore recommended that, at least initially, an outsider be used as an intermediary to create sufficient distance between him and the pupils and to allow pupils to be honest with their responses. He was aware that some pupils would be concerned about not hurting his feelings, and would want to avoid his developing a negative attitude towards them:

> *I don't know how well that would work because if the kids in the class like me, they won't want to upset me. If a kid in the class has had a bad lesson, they won't want to say.*

Mr Taylor, an experienced teacher at Greenfield, valued the aims of pupil consultation and thought he could use the evaluation sheets. Nevertheless, he was concerned about the consequences of such strategies in terms of time and commitment. To listen authentically to pupils would mean work on the evaluation reports:

> *I'd ... like to, given the time, I would like to have a complete record (of their comments) and so I could actually look at it ... I'd put it into a database and then say, 'OK, well John or Fred are constantly saying that this is not what they want'. Then I could actually identify that, or if there is a consistency across ... I mean I could analyse the data much more thoroughly. Yes, yes I mean I would actually, to have ... an afternoon or an evening, or a few hours, where I could actually say, 'Right OK, no it's time to look at this group' and I can then analyse the data ... then think about the week following and then see again how that's affected the following week.*

A form tutor at Mandela school also saw the value of learning about what worked in lessons. He thought that considerable skill is needed for such a strategy to work and, as he admitted, he was a total novice in terms of pupil consultation:

> *Never really done any apart from getting the fairly ad hoc – 'This is boring' – so, no, it's just not something I've done. It's just something I don't really take on board as a teacher. The most I've ever done in terms of Year 8 is 'Tell me what you've learnt today'. And if they can come back with it I'll think they're getting on fine.*

However, over the course of the four weeks, the evaluation sheets became increasingly productive. In the last week, when there was a clear pattern of the high-attaining boys expressing disturbing levels of negativity, he commented:

> *You see they're really like a silent four who I like enormously but occasionally I do actually take out all my frustration on them because they will be so quiet and then again I think they coast, won't push themselves. I think I could push them a lot harder. That's what I should be doing – as the kids are making loud and clear. I think you have to accept that sometimes you've misjudged the task and maybe haven't differentiated enough.*

Despite the welter of negative feedback, he believed that the evaluation sheets had been useful and enabling for pupils:

> *The less able kids, especially those who are slightly more diligent, loved it, especially little Ricky who just looked forward to them so much. Because there's the circling and a chance for evaluation. And you could see him concentrating and you know he loved being asked and that there was something to circle. Most of the others took time to think about it and were able to assess their own learning. They enjoyed the range of questions as far as I could see. But I could see they were focused on it. So I think they did it seriously and diligently.*

He was also able to identify positive aspects in terms of his own learning:

> I was a bit disconcerted because any teacher will claim it doesn't matter but of course we are all sensitive to evaluations and when I got the first batch – 'not at all interesting', 'not at all enjoyable', I was, 'Oh no' but I'd far rather see, know what they think. So it has been very, very interesting for me, actually, to be involved in this.

And this, in turn, has had positive repercussions for lesson planning:

> A couple of times they nearly all said 'boring' and they were right because we were just ploughing through stuff and it was boring. But then this last lesson I consciously thought 'liven it up' and they did a cut and paste exercise and various other things and, in fact, the feedback, you can see is a lot more positive so you could actually use it as a check.

The impact on teachers and on pupils suggests that if time and commitment were to be put into strategies of consultation, then there is much to be gained in terms of more effective teaching and learning.

Reflections and conclusions

Consulting pupils about the social conditions of learning in the classroom and how these social conditions relate to pupil learning can be painfully revealing, as we have seen. At the same time it can offer valuable insights into the impact of teaching on particular groups of pupils – their confidence as learners, about how far they feel included and valued in the learning process, and how much they feel in control over the content and pace of their learning (see also Rudduck and Flutter, 2004).

In this study we elicited a wide variety of pupil commentaries on social interactions in the classroom. There appeared to be strong motivation to learn amongst most pupils – even those whose experiences of classroom life were fraught with difficulty. Most pupils appeared to want to get on in school, to be noticed and helped by teachers to learn and to have some control over their learning. However, there was considerable diversity of experience and perspective between male and female pupils and between pupils from different social class and ethnic backgrounds. Pupil consultation strategies which focus on group discussions and formal feedback provide very different insights into classroom life in comparison with mentoring strategies with individual pupils. This diversity of pupil voice – the different ways of talking, the accounts of classroom life, the different perspectives on how the social dynamics work and affect their learning patterns – can inform teachers' work and extend their understandings of the potential of their practice.

Consulting pupils about the social conditions of learning and learning itself can:

- help develop greater understanding and awareness of progress
- help build trust between teachers and pupils and between social groups
- help provide greater possibilities for matching pupil needs and expectations with teaching strategies
- help yield information about how different groups of pupils experience and are motivated by particular lessons or topics
- help support teachers' self analysis of their own performance
- help identify strategies for eliciting those pupil voices which are not usually heard or which are excluded or undervalued in the classroom
- help expose social inequalities in the classroom that teachers may not always be fully aware of
- help teachers to engage more deeply with pupil needs in relation to learning, particularly in relation to their desire to be asked, listened to, respected and responded to in terms of their particular learning patterns and styles.

Our data also suggested that those pupils with interpersonal skills and the competence to communicate can successfully manipulate classroom learning in their favour. The group discussions, particularly with higher-achieving girls from upper middle class backgrounds, illustrated a capacity for independent learning as well as confidence in the classroom. But the social dynamics of the classroom for these pupils were not always easy, especially if they were called 'boffs', or were isolated or disliked for their success. Moreover, their strategies for gaining teachers' attention and help could be disrupted by the classroom strategies of disaffected or disengaged pupils, often boys. Consultation with these pupils can bring into the open their frustrations and needs.

Pupil consultation can have particular benefits for those pupils who are the least successful at learning. The discussions we held with lower-achieving pupils, often from working class backgrounds, allowed pupils to articulate how tense and vulnerable they felt in the classroom and how they tried to find ways of learning but had difficulty with so many aspects of classroom life. They did not feel trusted by teachers and were therefore not confident about asking for help. The discussions also uncovered how issues to do with seating, homework and teacher attention could be experienced as a form of regulation rather than as aids to learning. Working class boys appeared to see most classroom events in relation to their friendships and peer group cultures, which were major sources of identity and learning support. Friends and peer cultures had particular significance for them in the context of underdeveloped or dysfunctional relationships with teachers. As many said, being a good learner involved paying attention and getting on with the work – but talking to friends at the same time. Keeping both the social and the academic in balance was essential for pupils who were insecure about their learning.

Pupil consultation could potentially challenge taken-for-granted assumptions about learning processes which assume common standards of communicative competence and interpersonal skills. By exploring the power of pupil consultation for learning, teachers can reflect on the methods of communication usually employed in the classroom. Pupils were aware of the types of language needed to talk to teachers about learning and knew that there were inequalities in who can speak this language and be heard. By consulting groups of pupils, teachers could begin to encourage new types of relationships and new ways of talking with them – but the process of consultation itself is as important as the insights gained from pupils about the social aspects of classroom life.

4 Perspectives on classroom consultation

Donald McIntyre

We undertook the two research studies that we have reported in this book on the basis of two premises. One was that in principle consulting pupils about their teaching and learning must be good. Pupils are surely entitled at least to have their views listened to about how they spend a large part of their lives and about the kinds of learning activities which they find helpful. Furthermore, previous studies had suggested that pupils tend to have helpful things to say about teaching and learning. Our other premise, however, was that in practice consulting pupils about classroom teaching and learning might very well add to the complexity of the task of teaching, and therefore that it was important to understand the implications of consulting pupils.

The two studies were very different. One focused on teachers and on the implications for them of listening carefully to what their pupils had to say. The researchers sought the pupils' ideas about what teachers did helpfully and what they could do more helpfully. The whole study was conceived in terms of providing potentially useful pupil ideas for teachers. The other study focused instead on the social realities of pupils' classroom lives, and on aspects of classroom life likely to be important to the pupils but about which teachers might be relatively uninformed. While the first study, as it turned out, generated relatively consensual pupil views, the second study revealed, using the very different perspectives of different groups of pupils, how social inequalities shape classroom communication.

We shall discuss briefly some common themes which emerged from these two different studies and then the major contrast between them, before going on to consider the main lessons which we think can be learned about pupil consultation.

Some common themes

One of the strongest of the common themes was the concern of pupils to learn and to be helped to learn, and another was the thoughtful things that they had to say about what did and did not help their learning. In some cases, they may not have wanted to learn what schools had to teach them, but even in these circumstances they had sensible and useful things to say. The pupils wanted their teachers to understand their needs even if they didn't always find it easy to communicate these needs to their teachers.

Both studies also show very clearly the immense importance for pupils of the social world of the classroom. Learning, they wanted to tell us, is a social business. Social relationships among pupils are a major positive resource for learning, they were saying, a resource frequently neglected by teachers. At the same time, interactions among pupils can undermine learning in a variety of ways which teachers are not always aware of.

The basic human right of being treated like **people** was something that pupils frequently found it necessary to assert. They wanted to be treated with respect, both by their teachers and by their classmates, and in their experience the social conditions of the classroom – including teacher–pupil dialogue – were such as to make this uncertain. An important dimension of classroom life for many appeared to be vulnerability to embarrassment, and even humiliation. Having some control over their classroom lives and especially their learning was a pervasive concern; they valued even limited opportunities to make decisions about, for example, the pace of the work, where and with whom they sat, or what was worth recording from a learning experience.

Wanting to be trusted was another common pupil concern related to the desire for some control over their learning activities. Being consulted was itself much welcomed as an indication of trust, and pupils responded to the opportunity by demonstrating a quite remarkable trustworthiness to be serious rather than flippant and to be constructive rather than aggressive. Other indications of teacher trust were equally welcomed, but pupils were clear both that such trust was not something which they could rely on and also that considerable caution was necessary about trusting teachers, for example through being honest with them in commenting on their teaching.

Contrasting findings

The big difference between the two studies, partly in their designs but especially in their findings, related to the degree of consensus among pupils. The question of how much consensus can be assumed is of key importance for pupil consultation. The task of consulting pupils would be relatively easy if one could assume one common pupil voice but in many groups there are different voices that need to be heard.

The first of our two studies was therefore perhaps encouraging on this point. Not only did the pupils consulted give a clear consensual message about what are generally effective and preferred teaching and learning strategies, but also the message from these pupils was very similar to those of earlier studies, such as Rudduck et al (1996) and Cooper and McIntyre (1996). Irrespective of teacher, subject, school or their own previous academic success levels, pupils wanted teaching and learning activities offering depth of engagement, meaningful contextualisation, multimodal and active learning, and increased control over their own learning. On the general issues which are most obviously important for teachers, pupils seem to speak very largely with one voice. At the same time, they have helpful specific messages for specific teachers, reflecting their classroom experiences with these individual teachers.

The second of our two studies, which was concerned with the social realities of classroom learning, found no such consensus. Life in classrooms is very different for different kinds of pupils and can be especially different for pupils with different previous academic success levels and, closely related, for those from different social class backgrounds. And these differences interact in complex and important ways with pupils' gender and ethnicity. The study was designed to focus especially on pupils' feelings of confidence, inclusion and control, and in all these respects different kinds of pupils clearly had different kinds of classroom experiences and also different ways of conceptualising and assessing their learning and of communicating their needs to teachers. When one considers the central observations alongside the central importance for pupils of the social conditions of their learning, it becomes clear that pupil consultation, if it is to identify the learning needs of all pupils, will need to listen not just to what pupils have to say in common, but also to the multiple different voices themselves. Consultation strategies must work for those who are least successful in meeting the demands of schooling.

Lessons for pupil consultation

Our purpose in doing this research and in writing this book has been primarily to act as a conduit so that a wider audience can hear the voices of pupils when consulted and also the voices of teachers who have been helped to engage in consultation with their pupils. We believe that the main strength of this book is in the detail of the pupil and teacher voices it carries and that detail cannot usefully be condensed. What we can do here is distil from our findings a few simple truths about pupil consultation which we believe the research has shown.

First, we believe that it is abundantly clear, from this and earlier work, that pupils can offer their teachers much thoughtful, constructive and helpful commentary on life and learning in their classrooms.

It is also clear from our evidence that teachers can use pupil ideas to develop their teaching in ways which both they and their pupils believe are improvements.

Pupils cannot, however, be expected to do things that they have not had an opportunity to learn to do. As was explicitly elaborated in the second study, lower-attaining pupils tend to find it difficult to communicate to a teacher audience about what does and does not help their learning. Yet it is they who by definition most need to be able to explain their learning needs to teachers. Practice in doing so, and the reinforcement that would come from their ideas being used, would no doubt make a difference; but explicit guidance and supportive frameworks are also likely to be useful.

Having discovered how insightful and sensible their pupils' thinking about learning can be, teachers may be encouraged to move on to asking pupils to play fuller collaborative roles in planning and managing classroom learning. We have little doubt that this will be a key and very fruitful aspect of the future development of schooling; but again, pupils need to develop the expertise necessary for taking on such new roles. The challenge for teachers might be in recognising the need to plan for such new forms of collaboration.

Consulting pupils can mean very different things. In particular, the more time and thought given to it, the more informative and insightful the ideas shared are likely to be. But this does not mean that only in-depth approaches to pupil consultation are worthwhile. On the contrary, it is clear from both our studies that fairly simple consultation strategies – with individuals and with groups – can produce a lot of useful ideas; and it is probably sensible for schools and teachers to start with such simple strategies.

Nonetheless, it is clear that the more thought one invests in consulting pupils, the more productive it is likely to be. For example, methods of consultation which give pupils supportive guidance, but which also give them space to say what is important to them, are likely to be most valued. Our second study shows that many of the things that are most important to some pupils for their classroom learning might well be things that teachers would not usually ask them about, and also that the pupils who most need to be consulted about classroom learning are likely to be the most difficult to consult.

It was clear from our first study that pupil suggestions may often be attractive to teachers but yet seem to be at odds with other demands on them. Both the general business and complexity of classroom life and external curriculum and assessment requirements may make pupil ideas seem impractical or at best feasible only around the margins – for example, as end-of-term activities. It seems to us entirely understandable that teachers should react in such ways. Yet to do so is not to take pupil ideas entirely seriously. Furthermore, as the first study also showed, there are confident and skilled teachers who, despite other demands, can fruitfully assimilate both consultation procedures and the pupil ideas gained through these procedures into their practice.

Teachers interested in consultation strategies, but lacking experience, will need support from their school and the courage to face and learn from what can sometimes be uncomfortable knowledge. For all teachers who are developing consultation, it is important to be clear about purposes as well as strategies (see MacBeath et al, 2003; Fielding and Bragg, 2003).

Conclusion

Finally, we must conclude that consulting pupils about teaching and learning has an enormous amount to offer teachers; but consulting pupils is not at all straightforward. While we are confident that the benefits to be gained will justify the effort that engaging thoughtfully in pupil consultation will involve, it is individual teachers, departments and schools who would have to do the work who should make the decision.

Consulting pupils about teaching and learning is part of a wider impetus for change which we believe is, and certainly should be, welcomed into our schools: it is an important condition for, and is itself dependent on, the development of more collaborative ways of working in schools and more trusting relationships between teachers and all their pupils.

References

Arnot M, Gray J, James M and Rudduck J (1998) *A Review of Recent Research on Gender and Educational Performance*, OFSTED Research Series, The Stationery Office

Bernstein B (1977a) Social class, language and socialisation, in J Karabel and A Halsey (eds) *Power and Ideology in Education*, Oxford University Press

Bernstein B (1977b) *Class, Codes and Control*, Vol 3, Routledge

Bernstein B (1996) *Pedagogy, Symbolic Control and Identity*, Taylor and Francis

Cook-Sather A (2002) Authorising students' perspectives: towards trust, dialogue and change in education, *Educational Researcher*, 31, 4, 3-14

Cooper P and McIntyre D (1996) *Effective Teaching and Learning: Teachers' and Students' Perspectives*, Open University Press

Doyle W (1986) Classroom organisation and management, in M C Wittrock (ed) *Handbook of Research on Teaching*, 3rd edition, Macmillan, 322-431

Epstein D, Elwood J, Hey V and Maw J (1998) *Failing Boys? Issues in Gender and Achievement*, Open University Press

Fielding M and Bragg S (2003) *Students as Researchers: Making a Difference*, Pearson Publishing

Frosh S, Phoenix A and Pattman R (2002) *Young Masculinities*, Palgrave

Galton M, Gray J and Rudduck J, with colleagues (2003) *Transfer and Transitions in the Middle Years of Schooling (7-14): Continuities and Discontinuities in Learning*, HMSO

Gillborn D and Mirza H (2000) *Educational Inequality: Mapping Race, Class and Gender*, OFSTED, The Stationery Office

Gray J, Hopkins D, Reynolds D, Farrell S and Jesson D (1999) *Improving Schools: Performance and Potential*, Open University Press

Hey V, Creese A with Daniels H, Leonard D, Fielding S and Smith M (2000) Questions of Collaboration and Competition in English Primary Schools: Pedagogic Sites for Constructing Learning Masculinities and Femininities, ESRC project paper, Institute of Education, University of London

Jones B, Jones G, Rudduck J, Demetriou H and Downes P (2001) *Boys' Performance in Modern Foreign Languages – Listening to Learners*, CILT Publications

Lynch K and Lodge A (2002) *Equality and Power in Schools*, RoutledgeFalmer

MacBeath J, Demetriou H, Rudduck J and Myers K (2003) *Consulting Pupils: A Toolkit for Teachers*, Pearson Publishing

McIntyre D (2000) Has classroom teaching served its day?, in B Moon, M Ben-Peretz and S Brown (eds), *Routledge International Companion to Education*, Routledge

Nieto S (1994) Lessons from students on creating a chance to dream, *Harvard Educational Review*, 64, 4, 392-426

Reay D (2002) 'Troubling, troubled and troublesome': Working with boys in the primary classroom, in C Skelton and B Francis (eds) *Boys and Girls in the Primary Classroom*, Open University Press

Rudduck J, Chaplain R and Wallace G (1996) *School Improvement: What Can Pupils Tell Us?*, David Fulton

Rudduck J and Flutter J (2004) *How to Improve Your School: Giving Pupils a Voice*, Continuum Press

Sammons P, Thomas S and Mortimore P (1997) *Key Characteristics of Effective Schools*, Paul Chapman

Skelton C (2001) *Schooling the Boys: Masculinities and Primary Education*, Open University Press

Soo Hoo S (1993) Students as partners in research and restructuring schools, *The Educational Forum*, 57, 386-393, Summer

Willis P (1977) *Learning to Labour: How Working Class Kids Get Working Class Jobs*, Saxon House

Wright C, Weekes D and McGlaughlin A (2000) *"Race", class, and gender in exclusion from school*, Falmer Press

Younger M and Warrington M (1999) 'He's such a nice man but he's so boring. You have to really make a conscious effort to learn'; the views of Gemma, Daniel and their contemporaries on teacher quality and effectiveness, *Educational Review*, 51, 3, 231-241